UNANSWERED

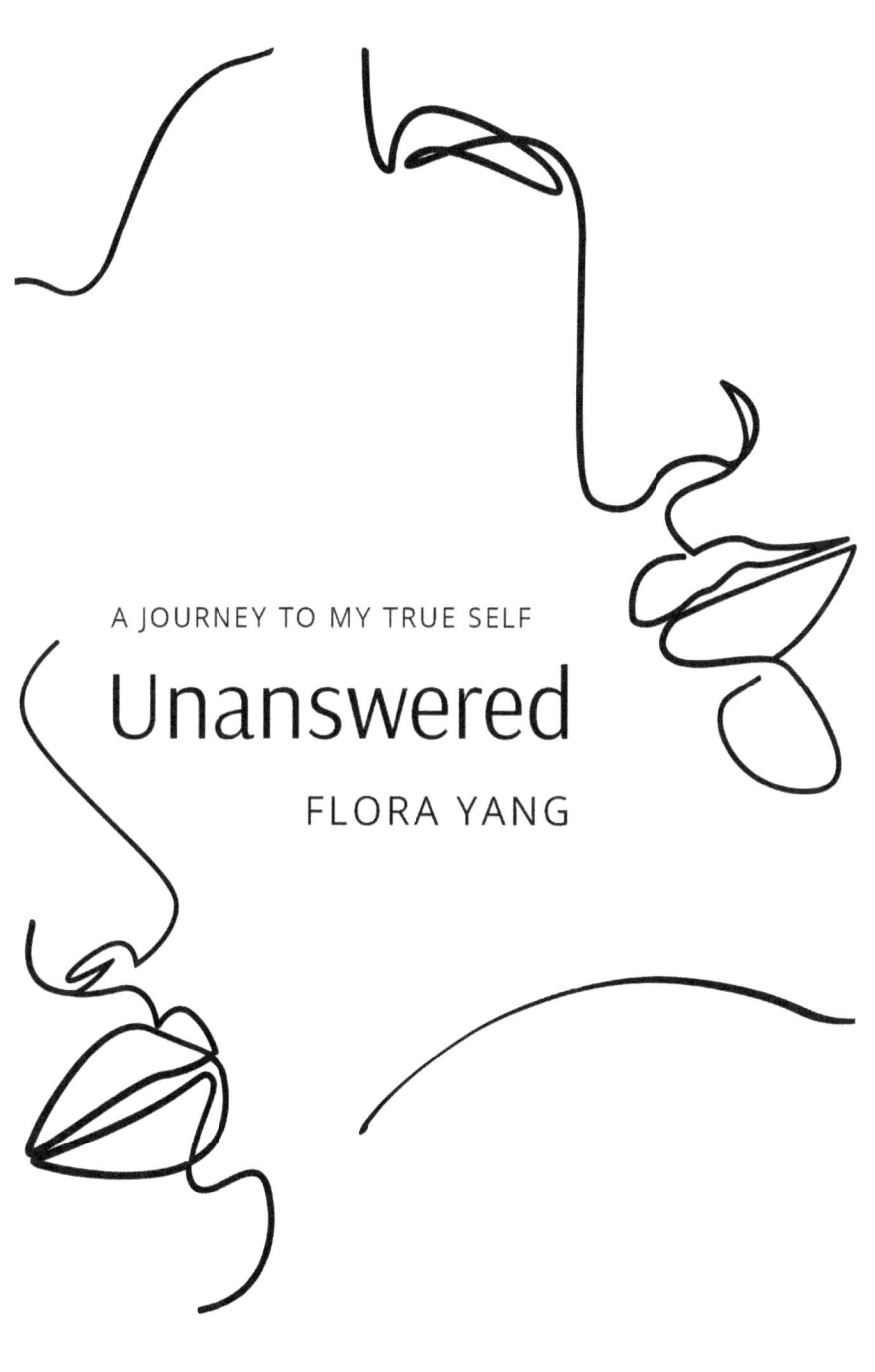

A JOURNEY TO MY TRUE SELF

Unanswered

FLORA YANG

NEW DEGREE PRESS

COPYRIGHT © 2021 FLORA YANG

All rights reserved.

UNANSWERED

A Journey to My True Self

Cover photo by Hammer Liu

ISBN

978-1-63676-496-2   *Paperback*
978-1-63730-415-0   *Kindle Ebook*
978-1-63730-416-7   *Digital Ebook*

To H.B.

You are loved.

CONTENTS

	AUTHOR'S NOTE	9
CHAPTER 1	UNANSWERED	13
CHAPTER 2	A TALE OF FIVE CITIES—KUNMING	19
CHAPTER 3	A TALE OF FIVE CITIES—BEIJING	25
CHAPTER 4	A TALE OF FIVE CITIES—SHANGHAI	33
CHAPTER 5	FORGET VS. FORGIVE	41
CHAPTER 6	A TALE OF FIVE CITIES—NEW YORK	57
CHAPTER 7	A TALE OF FIVE CITIES—VANCOUVER	71
CHAPTER 8	TIME ZONES	81
CHAPTER 9	WE CAN'T WRITE OTHERS' EXAMS	87
CHAPTER 10	WE GET WHAT WE HAVE	97
CHAPTER 11	MIGHT AS WELL JUST DANCE	107
CHAPTER 12	BLUE	113
CHAPTER 13	SECRET	119
CHAPTER 14	THE CAT BO LI	125
	ACKNOWLEDGMENTS	131
	APPENDIX	133

AUTHOR'S NOTE

Why did something so meaningful disappear so suddenly, so unexpectedly?

I was never given an answer. For years, I've been on a painful journey seeking answers but mostly searching clarity to one simple, deep, disturbing question.

Why?

Twenty years later, I still don't know why he didn't show up that day.

That was the first of many unanswered questions in my life. In the following years, there were more questions to come along—some answered, some that were never answered, and some that I let go of or I didn't want answers to. But during my most difficult times, it seemed there would never be light at the end of the tunnel. I didn't know what I could do except keep going. I wrote down my thoughts, day after day, and I wasn't sure if I would ever find what I was looking for. Today, as I flip through my old journals from those days, I can still see my tear marks on some pages.

What pulled me through those dark days were my learnings from Buddhism: everything that happened was supposed to happen, and everything that is supposed to happen would happen. I then started to realize "not happening" is a form of "happening," and in the same way, those "unanswered" questions were maybe a form of answer.

I started to let go of my clinging obsession to unanswered questions, but I still felt lost and didn't know what I was clinging on to. As I continued my path, I didn't know what I wanted, but I did know what I didn't want. In those moments I took the only path I could: seeking my true self and staying true to myself. I found validation in being my true self from time to time, such as getting the job I wanted, being admitted to my chosen MBA program, and finding my true love. I was without a doubt ecstatic to have these validating moments. However, when negative events occurred, I began to think I had failed, so I got frustrated and blamed myself.

After a bad bout of depression at the end of 2015, I realized that I was overwhelmed by consequences which were out of my control. My emotions fluctuated because I focused solely on the consequences. My learnings from Buddhism enlightened my thoughts that consequences become causes and causes could be a form of consequences, but the decisions that you make on your path are the only things that you have control over and the only things you can change. I started to realize that when I made decisions staying true to myself, I hadn't failed, regardless of the consequence.

I also finally realized that finding my true self and being true to myself was not a one-time project. As we cycle through cause to consequence to cause on our journey, we constantly have to seek ourselves and make the decisions that are the truest for us. We also have to put it into the perspective of our whole life's journey rather than any single, individual incident. As for me, the journey continues, and I can't wait to find out more about myself.

Writing is how I meditate, how I process my thoughts and my experiences, and how I continue reflecting and making connections. Every inch that we move forward will bring us a little bit closer to our true self, what we want, and where we are going. Ultimately, what's left to be fully owned by the end of the journey is the feeling we obtained from it. We will never have control over everything and may never like everything about ourselves, but we still have to embark on the journey of self-discovery to find peace, be content, and reach the Faramita (It refers to the *other shore* in Buddhism, meaning reaching the world of paradise through nirvana).

You could be in your early twenties feeling lost, mid-thirties facing a choice, or middle aged reflecting on the past, but the shared feeling of uncertainty binds us all together. Unlike other books claiming the utilitarian benefit, my book is not a panacea. It doesn't have all the answers, it doesn't guarantee a solution, but it will be with you, by your side, when you continue on your own journey to your true self.

CHAPTER 1

UNANSWERED

It had been six hours.

The twilight was shedding into total darkness—a typical spring afternoon in Beijing since the nights started early. I couldn't remember much about Beijing on that trip besides the wind.

I was still sitting on the swing seat by the window in the café next to the zoo. After standing outside of the zoo for about an hour, I had to move to stay warm. Swing seats by the window were their signature and an ideal spot: I could keep my eye on who was coming toward the zoo.

I called ZH's cell phone again using the landline at the café, but there was no answer. Cell phones were not a big thing in 2001, at least not for school kids, so I didn't have one and had to stay near somewhere with a phone. I left another message telling him I was still waiting but not in front of the zoo anymore, that I was sitting by the window of the café next door, and he should be able to see me right away. I didn't know how much more specific I could be. I was so worried that he couldn't find me, but later I understood: there were a hundred ways to find someone, the only way one couldn't was because one didn't want to. By the third bubble tea, I wasn't even sure I was still waiting.

I called another friend, Singhling, who I was supposed to meet the next day, asking if he would like to meet me at the café next to the zoo. I told him briefly about my situation, and he was kind enough to join me at the café. He arrived around 4 p.m., when I had been waiting for four hours. With his company, I wasn't even sure I was still waiting or what I was waiting for. We were chatting, but I was quite preoccupied by the fact that ZH had not shown up, returned my call, or notified me about it at all.

"Did you have any lunch while you were waiting?" Singhling asked.

"No I haven't. The plan was to have lunch with ZH, then hang out. But…" It's almost like as long as I didn't have lunch, there was still a chance he would show up.

"I see. It's about six o'clock. Shall we go and grab some food, and I take you back to your hotel? If he is not here by now, maybe…"

"Yes, I know, sounds like a good idea." Singhling was right and very considerate.

* * *

"You are back early!" My dad seemed a bit surprised when I got back to the hotel. He put down his book, got up from his bed, and walked to the desk to make me some hot tea.

"I thought you'd spend longer with ZH. How is he? How was your meeting? What did you have for dinner? Was it good? Did he bring you back?" He handed me the tea, sat down in the armchair, and looked at me wondering.

"No, Singhling brought me back. I had dinner with him." I sat down on the chair, leaning on the desk, holding my head exhausted. "He didn't show up today—at all."

"What? Why?"

"I don't know. I called him, left him messages, and waited for over six hours. I don't know why, and I don't care anymore."

"You should call him and ask. What if there is a misunderstanding?" My dad had always offered people the benefit of the doubt.

"What misunderstanding? He didn't show up, and that's it." I was really irritated and mumbling, trying not to take it out on my dad.

"No, you call him right now, here, ask him." My dad knew me quite well and was trying to help because he knew I would be haunted if I never tried to ask ZH.

"Why bother? He didn't show up. That means he didn't want to show up," I said as I started to lose it a little.

"You deserve an answer. He deserves an opportunity to explain himself. That's what friends do."

"I called him many times, and he didn't pick up! Maybe he didn't want to talk to me anymore or whatever."

But maybe I just didn't want to accept the fact that I was stood up by him.

Him. Why him? We knew each other since we were six years old at primary school and became close friends at fourteen. We exchanged letters every week for years after he moved to Beijing to pursue his violin academic life. I cherished his friendship so much. He was the one friend that had my back when I felt lonely after my parents got divorced. He was the one who comforted me when I was upset because my class teacher bullied me. He was the one who didn't judge me and was very protective when I told him that I was sexually harassed by my classmate. He was the one I hung out with and had so many good times with. He was the one who celebrated my application to a university in Beijing since we could meet up more.

He was also the one who, two months ago, told me that he liked me as more than just a friend and kissed my forehead. Why didn't he show up?

I was so excited to meet him in Beijing. The trip was for my interview for university admission, and for the first time, we were going to meet in somewhere else outside of our hometown, Kunming. It felt like we were grown up and independent. I wrote to him telling him the date of my interview, and we had a couple of calls before I left to arrange our meeting. He gave me his cell number, and we made the plan to meet up at the zoo for lunch and then go sightseeing. It was not the first time I visited Beijing, but it would have been so special if we were looking around together. I looked forward to it every day.

"Just call him and ask." My dad wasn't giving up. "It's so unfair that he stood you up like that. You should ask."

I called him, and he picked up this time.

"It's me, Flora." I was shivering.

"Oh, hi." He sounded startled. "I am sorry for today. Sorry I didn't show up."

"Why not?" My dad was right. I did want to know. I did want an explanation and a reason to stay friends.

"I am so sorry. Don't do this." He was nearly begging.

"I am not doing anything. I was asking you why you didn't show up. Just tell me." I wasn't upset, nor sad; I just wanted to know why.

"I am sorry, don't do this." He also called me by my secret name, the one only the two of us used in our letters.

"Do what?" I was getting irritated. "I am just wondering why you didn't come to the zoo."

"Don't do this. I am sorry. Please forgive me."

"I already did. I know you stand up people from time to time. But this time is a bit different. We made the plan a long time ago, and I was standing alone in the wind in front of the zoo. I waited for you for six hours. I just want you to tell me why you didn't show up. Were you sleeping and just didn't hear the alarm? Were you with someone else and forgot about our plan? Or what?" I was almost looking for an excuse *for* him.

"Please, don't do this. I am sorry." He didn't seem to be willing to give me an answer.

"ZH, we are good friends, and I am planning to keep it that way. Could you just let me know what happened that caused you to not show up, and we can call it a day?" I started to get really agitated to have to repeat this so many times.

"I am sorry."

I couldn't just hold the phone forever. I must have looked horrible because my dad was staring at me concerned.

"Okay, I am gonna go," I sighed. "This was our chance, and don't blame me for not giving us a chance." I hung up.

That was the last time we spoke to each other.

I was eighteen. Twenty years later, I still don't know why he didn't show up that day.

I still didn't know why such a close friend didn't even bother to find out how I was feeling. How could he just walk away from our friendship and possible blooming relationship? He didn't even seem to care about leaving me waiting in the cold wind for hours in a strange city.

How could something so meaningful disappear so suddenly? I was never given an answer.

For as long as I can remember, this sudden loss of our friendship has haunted me. Questions about this day have lingered…unanswered.

CHAPTER 2

A TALE OF FIVE CITIES—KUNMING

"Flora, did you have any plans for dinner?" My dad called me.

"No, I'm home. Are you not coming back?"

I went back to Kunming for the winter term break in 2004. As break normally went from mid-January till March, and Chinese New Year was usually in late January or sometime in February, I would just go home for a family reunion.

"No, I am going to have dinner with a bunch of friends. We are having hot pot. If you don't have anywhere to go, why don't you just join us?"

I knew my dad wanted to spend more time with me but didn't want to push too hard, so he involved me as much as possible in his social life. It was very common in my family that both my brother and I were involved in our parents' social lives. We had met many of their friends, and they knew us well. Meanwhile, our parents knew our friends too. They always encouraged us to introduce our friends to them, mostly for the sake of knowing who we were hanging out with.

However, I never expected that this dinner would begin a relationship that overshadowed me for ten years.

"Who do I know? I don't want to just come and eat."

"Right, your godfather is here. You haven't seen him since you came back. Why don't you just come over? If you don't have any other plans."

"Okay, I will come over." I didn't have anywhere to be, and it had always been pleasant to see my godfather occasionally.

It was close by, and the weather was warm. Kunming was known for its warm sunshine during winter. In fact, Kunming was known as "the Spring City." It is 1,890 meters above sea level but in the shape of a basin, so it has been endowed with impeccable weather, being cool in summer (around 28 degrees Celsius) and warm in winter (rarely below 0 degrees Celsius). So I walked over.

There were two other people there when I arrived. I hugged my godfather and greeted one of the men I'd never met. In China, we call nonrelatives of the same generation as our parents uncles and aunties.

"Hello, Uncle!"

"Hello! Welcome home. Heard so many great things about you from your father."

"Ahhh, thank you." I was slightly embarrassed. Parents always embarrassed us by telling too many great things about us to their friends.

"This uncle is the one I've mentioned before who I work with. He is very capable and smart." My dad turned to another man I'd never met.

When my dad was trying to introduce XM, I couldn't bring myself to call him uncle. I was in a bit of a trance. He was different from all my father's friends or even typical middle-aged men. He wasn't married and had no children.

He was tall and fit with long legs. He had a great temperament, with his hair mottled gray and black. His eyes were always sparkling, as if they belonged to a young boy without much life experience who was very curious about life. He was wearing a Chinese-style cotton-padded jacket with knotted buttons; it looked very special and not at all tacky.

"You will want to learn from him. He used to be a lawyer and investor in the United States. You love New York, don't you? He lived in New York for many years. Ask him about it!" My dad kept going on introducing him.

I was slightly embarrassed again because asking random people random things about New York seemed a bit stupid. I thought my dad did that because, in his mind, I was always the little girl that needed his guide for learning opportunities, but I was twenty.

"I heard you like New York."

He talked to me in English. His voice was grounded, warm, and humble. His English accent was very beautiful. I loved New York because of *Sex and the City*, but it didn't seem to be appropriate to talk about it in front of them.

"Yes, I learned more about New York recently." It felt weird to converse with him in English in front of a bunch of people speaking Chinese.

"*Nu* York."

"I am sorry?"

"New Yorkers will pronounce it *Nu* York. You sound more like a West Coaster."

I felt slightly ashamed as I didn't think that was something to be corrected on, so I laughed it off. We didn't have much more conversation that I could remember that evening.

I could tell my dad recognized XM as a positive influence. I admired my dad, so when he complimented someone,

I naturally trusted his judgement. I left with a very good impression of XM but nothing more than that.

Two days later, XM called me. I was quite surprised. I didn't know how he got my number—obviously from my dad, but using what reason? I didn't expect him to call me either. Why?

"I have two friends from New York coming to visit, and I arranged lunch with them tomorrow. But I am not feeling very well, could you join us? Maybe you can help out a little."

I was flattered that he considered my English good enough to help entertain his friends from New York. I was flattered that such a high-level talented man would consider involving me in his business and that he took the initiative to contact me.

I went for the lunch and realized he wasn't so sick that he couldn't talk. I was totally ignorant about what was really going on as I respected him as someone who was capable, smart, and had a lot of interesting life experience. I learned more about him firsthand from his stories, and he was everything but dull at that lunch.

He told us that he was invited to a party for the first time after he arrived to law school in the United States, but he didn't have any decent clothes except the suit assigned to him and a set of silk pajamas as a "diplomatic" gift just in case. So he decided to put on the silk pajamas and go to the party. The crowd was pleasantly shocked. People were curious about him because it was very rare in the 80s to see a Chinese guy studying in the United States, and it was even more rare that a Chinese student would come to a party so boldly, so unconventionally, and so much different than the stereotypes they had believed about China.

He was a good storyteller, not only because his experiences were so special but because when he was talking to people, his passion was infectious. His points of view were always insightful and unorthodox, never following the herd but also not just for the sake of being unique, which showed how smart and thoughtful he was. I couldn't resist his wisdom. He was so charismatic, and I was filled with admiration.

He called me again a few days later to have dinner together after work. I was aware of how busy his schedule was, so I couldn't help but get a bit dizzy that such a successful, powerful, and outstanding person would want to hang out with me. We met up a few more times, sometimes with his business partners, his friends, and so on, but they all somehow knew my father as well because it was a small city and they had overlapping circles. So I deemed it as a normal social interaction.

We had fun, and he kept telling jokes that weren't cheesy and looked at me searching for my laugh. The whole time he respected me and maintained proper limits between us, so him pursuing me was the last thing in my mind. In retrospect, I wasn't sure for a long time if he was just being a courteous respectful man or if he actually liked me in particular.

During this time when I was in my twenties, I was at an early stage of self-discovery where I focused on my ego. I was more concerned with how others viewed me than what I thought about myself. I wasn't focused on my own identity, and I was constantly looking for validation from others—from people I looked up to, I cared for, or that I admired. It is inevitable in the journey of self-discovery that we rely on role models. They can be anyone, and without sufficient self-awareness or knowing about our true self, they can come across dazzling and overwhelming, and we can be easily confused. That would lead to self-doubt, lower self-esteem, and getting lost, just like a boat shipped into the ocean before having its helm set, which can end up drifting or, even worse, being gobbled up by the dark ocean.

When the spring term started on March 1, I went back to Beijing.

CHAPTER 3

A TALE OF FIVE CITIES—BEIJING

Spring in Beijing was usually quite unpleasant.

It was still cold, yet the central heating usually stopped around mid-March. Then the haze would linger for as long as possible until it got blown away by the spring wind, which felt like a knife cutting on your cheek. The sky stayed gray for days until the real spring came, and when it did, it got humid and warmer. Then the willow and aspen catkins started fluttering in the air, everywhere. If you opened your mouth outside carelessly, you would inhale the catkins and cough.

Not long after I got back to Beijing from Kunming after my winter vacation, I received a phone call.

"Hi Flora, it's XM."

His voice was as grounded, as warm, as humble as I remembered. Because I majored in English broadcasting and was trained in accents and vocal performance, I was extra sensitive to voice and accent. He was originally from Beijing, so his accent was perfect when speaking Chinese.

"Oh! Hello!" I still couldn't bring myself to call him uncle. I didn't know why. Hopefully, that didn't come across rude to him, I thought to myself.

"I am back in Beijing today for a couple of meetings. I remembered you are studying in Beijing, right?"

"Yes." I had so much going on in my mind, but I couldn't talk more.

"Right, I am not staying long this time but would like to find a time to come to see you, see if you need anything. Your dad always talks about you and cares about you. Since I am here anyways, might as well just check in."

His actions were all very appropriate. Sometimes my dad would ask his friends who traveled to Beijing to bring me some local food to satisfy my cravings or simply to check in on me. It's more of a convenient favor rather than trouble.

"Oh, thank you." I didn't know what to say.

"Where are you?"

"Beijing Broadcasting Institute…"

"Um…"

"Outside of the 5th Ring Road East!"

"Right, I thought so. I am around Northwest, 5th Ring as well. The traffic would be like hell. Is there any transportation convenient for you to get closer to downtown?"

"I can take the subway to the Trade Center, next to 3rd Ring Road East."

"That will do! Do you have class this afternoon?" He still needed to drive through two-thirds of the city to meet me.

"No, I don't." I was usually very talkative, but with him, I was always very succinct.

"Are you able to get to the Trade Center around two o'clock? We can have a coffee."

"Sure."

"See you later! Bye."

He looked just like what I remembered from a few weeks ago—spirited, dapper, and well attired. We sat down in a coffee shop near the World Trade Center. I didn't want to take much of his time. *Wait*, I thought to myself, *he asked me out.*

He was smoking while we were talking. I really didn't like people smoking, but I didn't say anything simply because I didn't think we were close enough to be able to say it out loud.

He was well-spoken, decent, and tactful. He asked about my school life, if I needed any stationary or books, how the food around campus was, and so on…all trivial stuff. While answering those questions, I got more and more confused about why he paid a visit given he didn't stay long in Beijing and had a busy schedule. In those very few occasions when my father's friends visited, it was when they were nearby or convenient; XM seemed to prioritize seeing me over the other things he needed to do. Why did he drive all the way across the biggest city in China to chitchat with me?

He might have had some agenda, but I was so dense with him from the beginning since I didn't believe someone so successful, experienced, smart, or out of my league in many ways would like me the way he did. I was 20, had no idea about life, and had little to offer. Years later, I realized there are different types of "attraction" and "relationships." What was he looking for? I was never clearly told, but as time passed by, I was clearer about what I always wanted. I wanted true love: heart, soul, and respect with his whole being.

After a while, the man at the next table stood up, walked towards the entrance, and was about to leave. He was very tall and well-built, wearing a red hoodie and sports pants. It was hard not to notice him. XM and I both stopped talking at the same time and gazed at him while he passed by our table outside the window. Our eyes followed him as he was walking toward his car as we were both curious about what kind of car he was driving. Then he wormed into the tiniest sports car in the world, which looked completely out of proportion with his tall build. It was just funny.

XM and I looked at each other and grinned at the same time. I could tell he was all lit up, maybe because it was quite funny, maybe because he saw me relax and smile. I was surprised that we had this serendipity. I started to know more about him—not just as my father's friend, not as a successful businessman, not as someone else, but as him.

* * *

When it was getting humid and warm, the summer in Beijing started.

XM came back to Beijing almost every other week and always drove across the city to take me to dinner. We spent hours talking—or, rather, me listening to him talking. I was so fascinated by his stories. Ah, those fascinating stories! He once told me when he was serving as an Air Force pilot, he was chosen to be an interpreter but knew zero English. So he studied nonstop for three months. He told me about how he went to the United States to study law and became a lawyer when he felt stuck as an officer in the Trading Bureau. He was negotiating deals in Washington, DC, for four hours, and on the flight back to New York, his brain literally shut down resulting in him losing speech for a couple of hours. Those were not necessarily soul-stirring stories, but for me back at that time, they were just fascinating.

I also liked the story of his pet bird, named Old West. The bird always jumped on his shoulder to greet him and paced a little, and as he told this story, he used his fingers mimicking the bird walking on my shoulder. I was always smiling listening to his stories. He was such a good storyteller, and I was always engaged, laughing, worrying, or empathizing with the story line.

With so much going on in my mind, I didn't talk much. I was like a still pond on the outside with a river of euphoria inside. Only ten years later, when we broke up for the last time, did he complain, "You have never talked about what was on your mind, never told me what you want." Nobody else had ever claimed that I kept to myself. Maybe that was an indicator that I wasn't entirely being myself most of the time around him.

For the whole early summer, I wandered around with him. When I was with him, time seemed to flash by while also stopping simultaneously. Frankly, I was lost in our time together. And every time after he left, I missed him so much that it hurt. I even had a fever in June as if my body couldn't handle such strong emotion.

"Hi Flora, it's XM! I am back."

It was in July, right before my summer vacation. I planned to go home right after my exam, and I was very touched that he managed to still come to see me shortly before that.

"How long are you going to stay?" I was trying not to be too excited.

"A few days. I am in a couple of meetings, but do you have any plans for dinner tonight? I would like to pick you up to have dinner. And we can go and check out this bar run by my nephew at Hou Hai." Hou Hai was a beautiful lake located in the centre of Beijing which used to be part of the royal garden, but nowadays, it is one of the most visited areas in the city.

"Sure. Whenever." I couldn't wait to see him.

I have always tended to be both accommodating and understanding. I was respectful of others' time sometimes more than mine back then. When people portrayed themselves as being busy, I tended to "not take time from them." Looking back, I was sending signals that I didn't think I was important enough to take up other people's time. If people spent time with me, I would interpret that they were willing to do so. Being empathetic and respectful about others' time was part of who I was, but I also improved to be less apologetic when I "take time" from other people.

That evening wasn't so hot, and the dusk brought a breeze rippling across the surface of the lake. We were sitting outside of his nephew's bar facing the lake and chatting as usual after we finished dinner. He then went to his car and opened the trunk, bringing over a basket of lychee while asking his nephew to rinse them so we could have some.

"These were just delivered before I came to pick you up," he mentioned casually.

"Oh, from where?"

"From the orchard we own in Dong Guan—" a tropical city in Guang Dong Province, famous for lychee and other tropical fruits. "I asked the staff to harvest some this morning and send them over via flight so that we could have them fresh tonight! You know, the fresher the better. I would like you to get the best taste as they are very good."

His nephew was quite surprised and kept complimenting the lychee. I was surprised and also felt like there must be more to his rush to have the lychee delivered the same day. There is a well-known story about an Emperor in ancient China, who loved one of his concubines so much that he spoiled her by abusing the military horse courier system to bring lychees to her - just because she liked them. So when the fruit was ripe, it took many riders riding horses nonstop to deliver it freshest due to the geographical distance as well as the fruit's delicacy.

While my thoughts were drifting away, I had a few of them. But the lychee was very juicy, so my fingers got sticky and messy. After a few of them, I went to the washroom then came back with clean hands, so I stopped eating them.

"Why stop? Such good lychee," he asked.

"Oh I just wanted to take a break. Don't want to get my fingers messy again so soon." I smiled.

He then started to peel them for me and hand them over. I was overwhelmingly flattered.

When he dropped me off in front the dorm building, I really didn't want to leave him but had to. We were sitting in the car, paused for a little and said goodbye. Then I reluctantly turned to the door to get out, he gently tapped my elbow and said "sweet dreams" in English.

I turned back to look at him, lit up. He must have seen it and smiled back. I then jumped out of his SUV and went back to my dorm. I didn't look back walking across the garden, but I didn't hear the car driving away either. I could only hear my heart beating like a drum.

I had dreams that night. I didn't know if they were sweet, but sometimes, love would not always be sweet.

CHAPTER 4

A TALE OF FIVE CITIES—SHANGHAI

I've always wanted to live in Shanghai.

During my summer vacation in 2002, I visited Shanghai for the first time. It was so humid and hot, but the trip to the city just reconfirmed my love of it. My hometown of Kunming was nowhere near Shanghai, so it usually took more than three hours to fly from one to the other. The food, the weather, and the city vibe were all very different, but I liked Shanghai so much that I thought of it as my second hometown. Maybe because my favourite author Eileen Zhang lived in Shanghai for most of her life or maybe because in the books and movies, Shanghai had always been an exciting place and full of trends. Maybe because it was the city where the modern and the old, the West and the East, merged together.

In comparison to Beijing, Shanghai was recognized as the economic center of China, so it was more modern, vibrant, and flexible. As the political and cultural center, Beijing had its own charm, but it wasn't entirely for me. I never got used to the weather even after four years of university. The food portions were just way too big for me. The city was too spread out and always felt heavy and gray. I just couldn't envision my life there. When I finished university, I was ready to move away.

"Why don't you come back to Kunming?" The first time XM asked me this question was in the summer of 2004.

"I don't see any opportunity for me there." Truth was, I was twenty-one, and the world was too big. I didn't want to go back home yet.

"You can work at the TV station. Aren't you supposed to be a TV presenter? It's also easier for me to see you. Or just stay in Beijing. I come back a lot."

"I don't really like Beijing." What I kept to myself was that I had a secret worry that if I didn't keep exploring, I would never have the chance to. Kunming was a laid-back city, slow in development and mindset. I didn't want to retire just yet.

I had a secret worry that I would end up mostly just being available for him, waiting for him, and that I wouldn't have my own life—that if I went back to be with him, soon we wouldn't be together anymore, that he would never confirm what we were, so I would forever be in a limbo situation.

It was quite awkward that he and my father shared a lot of acquaintances in such a small city. Too many. I didn't want to put my father in a difficult situation. He was devastated when I told him that I was in love with XM. He mumbled, "How could he…" He then phased out working with him. It was obvious that he wasn't supportive but didn't force me to do anything so the least I could do was not to show up in front of his other friends.

Looking back, I didn't have much of a rationale, but I just followed my heart.

"You should just come back with me." This was the last time he visited me in Beijing. He was staring at me so deeply that I couldn't look back but shied away.

"We don't have a chance in Kunming." I sighed. He didn't respond.

I wasn't sure what that was. I was never assured of what we were exactly as he never made things "straight" between us. Yes, we hung out while he visited Beijing or when I was back home almost every day, but it was always on his time. I was so hopelessly obsessed with him that I didn't expect anything else other than just to see him. Yes, I knew he was busy, so I was always waiting for him to call because I never wanted to "bother" him.

I was pretty sure he wasn't entirely single either. There were multiple female friends of his who would hang out with us from time to time who I could tell, from the first sight, were involved intimately with him. I had a secret worry that I would just become another woman to him.

He never explained, never tried to make it clear, which made me wonder if he was enjoying it somehow. He never held my hand, never hugged me, let alone kiss me or anything else. He always introduced me as "Yang's daughter" when meeting with his friends. But he kept calling, seeing me, and taking me to dinners and weekend trips. It didn't feel right in my heart, but I couldn't tell what exactly was wrong.

Though I felt a consistent vague disquietude, I was so addicted to the moments that touched my heart so deeply that they sent shivers up my spine.

Once we went to the mountain he owned. After dinner we went for a walk outside of the villa. His friends came as well, but they were back inside to prepare BBQ. It became quiet with just the two of us, a light breeze and the ink-dark sky above. We were strolling slowly, and he suddenly pulled me close to a tree and said, "Ya'ya, listen…the tree is talking." My eyes immediately filled with tears.

The other time we went to a hot spring on a cold night right before Chinese New Year. He just managed to finish working last minute, and he was quite tired. The resort was almost empty, and we were having a walk after dinner. He suddenly said, "Ya'ya, why don't we just move to a lodge in the mountain and live a peaceful life together, far away from all this noise." My heart was screaming yes, but I couldn't say a word. I knew this would not happen no matter how much I wished.

Once we ran out of ideas after dinner, I took him to watch a movie. He was reluctant at first, but I talked him into it as the movie was produced by the production house where he was a shareholder. The last time he had watched a movie at a cinema was about ten years prior. The next day he went to the office and couldn't stop talking about going to see a movie—just like a boy.

He told me that shortly after he moved back from the United States, his mom fell sick and was sent to hospital for a surgery. He had heard that to make sure the patient was treated with more care, the patient's family needed to send gift to the doctors. Hoping she would get the best possible treatment, he sent an envelope full of cash to the doctor via a friend. The doctor was so spooked because this friend was quite powerful and, more importantly, the envelope was too big. The doctor became paranoid that someone with this amount of power and money could also easily blame him and impact his life if anything went wrong, so the doctor decided to take the conservative treatment.

"I screwed up. I screwed up the chance to save her." I doubted it has anything to do with that, but he blamed himself all the time.

It was the first time I saw him so sad that he was almost crying. Showing vulnerability can be hard for anyone but definitely harder for a man like him, and him doing so in front of me made me believe that I, us, our relationship meant something to him.

For those times, the only way I could respond was with tears in my eyes, feeling the emotion welling up inside threatening to overwhelm me. I was always looking for the next validation, and when they came, I clung to them.

We became really temperamental after the first time we slept together. It wasn't any good, but he made it worse afterwards.

"Did you know what that was? Incest."

He didn't seem to be happy at all, and it seemed like he almost regretted it. But why did he say that to me? He made it sound like I was responsible, like only I performed the activities.

"Do you know what incest is? We are not related!" I was furious.

That was the first time I remember ever arguing with him. I was so pissed that I not only had bad sex but that I also had to deal with this bullshit. It was a sign. Back in my early twenties, I didn't think sex was very important, though I was always curious about it. It was important, especially as a factor to assess the compatibility between two people.

I believed he felt for me; I just didn't know how much or in what way. I believed we had our chance. We just didn't manage to seize it. I believed we both acted in good faith. Maybe it was just not the right timing. Like the first time I told him I loved him, he shook his head and said, "Don't say things like that." Even as I wanted to be a moth flying toward the fire, the flame was flickering.

***

I decided to move to Shanghai in February of 2006 when I got a job offer at an industrial magazine. Love and life—if I wasn't able to control one of them, at least I could try to control the other. I told him, and he didn't say anything.

"Hi Flora, it's XM!" Shortly after I moved, I received a call from him.

"Oh, hi!" I was excited, still.

"I moved my March board meeting to Shanghai, and I'm just finishing. Did you want to join us for dinner tonight?"

"Of course!" I was very touched. It must have had something to do with me, even a little, right?

I took a cab to the gallery. There was a beautiful patio on the top of this art deco building in the town center of Shanghai. They were already there chatting at the bar.

He was even better looking than I remembered. It was the first time I saw him in business casual (Western style). His blazer and pants were woollen in charcoal gray with very fine silver stripes. He was wearing a black cashmere turtleneck. Even more rare, he was wearing a pair of very decent Oxfords.

I said hello to his partners from his law firm in New York. One of them brought his wife, and she was a typical Upper East Side lady, fitting every description from the movies. She greeted me, "Oh so this is your Flora? So nice to meet you!"

I was overwhelmingly flattered.

"What did you tell them about me?" I asked when we were back to his hotel.

"Nothing unusual." He didn't seem to want to open up more. "So what do you think about Shanghai after living here for over a month?"

"I like it! So sophisticated and modern."

"I don't find it good at all! It's so phoney and empty. Crazy buildings everywhere. I think Beijing has more flavour. You should consider going back to Beijing or coming back to Kunming." He said it again.

I got a bit defensive but didn't want to argue with him. It's fine he preferred Beijing, but how about understanding my preference as well? I gradually realized that even though he could behave perfectly, deep down he was very uncomfortable with the Shanghai style, which some would consider "too material."

He was born in a military family where his father was a general of the national air force and was very strict with the four of them. His older brother and sister were very obedient. One of the examples he told me was they got married to someone assigned to them; his younger brother wasn't strong-minded either.

He was an exception, always the troublemaker and head of the herd of kids in the neighborhood. Still, since he grew up in a military officers' compound, hung out with peer boys, and spent a chunk of time in the military, there was never room for emotion, sensitivity, or enjoying life from a material level. "Enjoy life" was probably not even a thing in his mind or at least defined very differently from my terms.

After his service as an Air Force pilot, he moved to a job in translation. He studied English nonstop for three months and was able to work as a translator. He then started to work in the foreign trade sector and was one of the first overseas students dispatched by the state after Nixon's visit to China. He worked very hard to finish his law degree and became a lawyer in New York.

After making partner, he started to work in investment banks then moved back to Southwest China to run a part of the family business created by his siblings. He was seasoned in New York as a lawyer and investment banker. He adapted well with whatever was required in terms of appearance, behavior, or manners, but that was never his comfort zone.

We had a very fundamental divergence on the idea of quality of life. We later found this out, but back then we didn't know as we never lived together. I just thought it was as simple as northerners didn't like southerners, and he maybe thought it was as simple as I was a young girl who loved vanity.

I was hopeful about our relationship for the first time as I could hold his arm and walk down the street openly without worrying about being seen. I thought Shanghai could be a turning point for our relationship if we both worked on it. But he stopped coming to Shanghai just because he didn't like it there, as if I was never a factor. I got disheartened as he called me less and less. What about all the good old times? How could something so meaningful disappear just like that?

I was sad but not ready to resign. I dated around but wasn't serious. Without being sure about myself, even a toxic relationship could be considered a "part of myself" that I needed. As if by still being "in love" with him, I could defeat any other pain, even though that pain was actually caused by how f*cked up this very relationship was. That was wrong.

There is no such thing as beautiful pain. Pain is pain, and we should stop it as soon as possible. There can be lessons to learn or reflections to have, but there will never be anything to gain by holding on to the pain. I wish I could have learned this sooner, but back then I was so desperately attached to this twisted relationship.

CHAPTER 5

FORGET VS. FORGIVE

―

I was flipping through my journals from 2007 through 2009. Page by page, the entries were relatively vague and mostly just descriptions of my feelings rather than what was going on during that time. However, I didn't need the journals to remind me of all the anger, fear, despair, and shame that were so alive at my fingertips. Just seeing the words I jotted down brought them back.

Yet I forgot. I forgot about what had happened fully. It's weird that I remembered some of the fragments so vividly, yet others were obscured. Like looking through a veil, I could not clearly reproduce them in my mind.

So my writing wasn't helpful for ranting or memory. Why did I write?

Among all the keenly felt pain, what bothered me the most was…shame. When I was trying to identify my emotions after it all happened, I couldn't push the sense of shame out of my mind. Yes, I was angry about the way I was treated. Yes, I was scared when he threatened to burn down my house. It was my home as well as a historical building. Yes, I was desperate, and it seemed there was no way out. So much so that at a point I thought of maybe ending my life. But why shame?

It was not long after I moved to Shanghai. Menoetius and I met because my friend Amanda was setting up a blind date for another girlfriend of ours, Donna. She was very shy and didn't want to make it all about her or super awkward, so she asked both me and Amanda to go with her. Menoetius was a colleague of Amanda's boyfriend, Lewis, at that time. We were all a similar age and working in the same industry, so there weren't any obstacles to basic trust, and Lewis also said good things about him. What could go wrong?

We all met up for dinner in May 2007. He was quite good looking and also very spirited. The conversation went well among all of us. He was open about the fact that he was from a small village and had never gone to college. When he talked about work with Lewis, we could tell he was very hardworking and trying his best to advance. He was also very good with people as he worked as account manager for his company. Overall Menoetius came across refined, courteous, and, most importantly, normal.

Amanda and Lewis left after dinner, but when I got up to leave, Donna insisted that we take the bus together. I understood and agreed as we were single girls living alone in a big city, and safety was the top priority. If she didn't feel like it was safe to be left alone with anyone, then she shouldn't be. We all took the bus together and said goodbye just fine, but before splitting, we all connected over MSN. (In case young readers are wondering, MSN was one of the first few online chatting tools developed by Microsoft. It was also connected to Myspace.)

Then I went to Cannes, France, for a business trip. After I came back, one day Menoetius reached out to me over MSN.

"Hi, how was France?" he messaged.

"Not bad! I was so excited! It was the first time I went to France and got to see Paris."

We exchanged a bunch of messages. He asked if we could meet for dinner sometime. I was a bit confused as I thought he was dating Donna.

"Hahaha, no, no." Donna laughed. She told me and Amanda that she wasn't really interested.

So I thought it would be okay to meet him alone for dinner as friends. We chatted about my trip and had another good conversation with a friendly ending. Then he started to message me every day but not in a pushing way. Of course, I could tell he wanted to be more than friends, but my mind wasn't in the right place. When we went out again, I told him directly that I was preoccupied by a man who I then considered to be the love of my life. He didn't seem to be upset or anything, instead he was quite understanding and comforted me a little.

I was swamped in the twisted confusion and pain from my relationship with XM. I was not in a good place for my own mind, let alone any relationship. It was like floundering in a dark lake with water weeds tangled around my ankle. Many years later, I was blessed to realize that it was not entirely in my control to deal with this feeling, but back then I wasn't self-aware enough to realize that.

Menoetius and I started dating just casually. I vented a lot about my swamped situation with him so he was very aware what was going on in my life. I thought I made it clear that I didn't want to have a serious relationship. I was so naive.

The first time I started to feel antipathy toward him was when we were talking about work. I was quite busy back then, but I loved my job.

He once joked, "Why do you keep rolling? No matter how good a woman is at work, she will always get married and take care of the family."

I was a bit surprised but didn't judge him. His idea of a woman's role was absolutely against what I believed in, but I was brought up with an open mind, not judging people from a different or opposite perspective. Many years later I learned to feel very free to judge not because I became judgmental, but because I became more aware of my true self. But back then, I just thought everyone deserved to have one's own opinion.

"Well really? Not me anyways. I don't think I want to get married."

"You will one day. You just don't realize it yet. You are just saying smart things." So I was the one who got judged?

"As long as the day doesn't come, I don't." Why was he telling me about myself? My instinct was to be offended, but I couldn't identify why exactly. Later on I realized that it was a violation of who I am.

He laughed and dropped the topic. I wasn't sure if he was convinced or understood that we didn't share the same opinion, but I didn't bother to find out, simply because I didn't care. What was the point in arguing with someone who had the opposite point of view and didn't want to listen?

The moment I decided not to continue our relationship was during a trip to the water park a few months after we started dating. We rented a kayak with a deposit. It was a typical summer day of Shanghai—crazy hot, humid, and sticky. One can't possibly stay out of the water. The park was packed. When we got back from swimming to the parking area, we found a bunch of identical kayaks. He grabbed one and tried to bring it back to the return. A middle-aged woman stopped him.

"Wait, this is my kayak," she yelled.

"No it is mine. I parked here." He was trying to leave but became defensive.

"What are you talking about? There are others, go get those. Don't steal mine." She reached out to grab the rope.

He fought back, and they started to pull and push, cursing at each other. That was one of the most embarrassing moments in my life. I hated that I was associated with someone like that. I hated to make a public scene while having to watch a young man physically fighting with a middle-aged woman. I was so embarrassed that I didn't even go up and try to stop it. I was standing away, waiting for it to end.

I was speechless. He failed to snatch the kayak, so we didn't have one to return and cursed all the way to the cashier. I explained the situation and told the manager that it was identical to others so it wasn't only our responsibility. Besides, the water park was guarded so anyone who even tried to walk out with a kayak would have been spotted. We finally got the deposit back. He was still very upset. In retrospection, he must have observed that I wanted to avoid conflict or drama, and he apparently had no problem taking advantage of it. He always lashed out when things didn't go his way, and I would try to compromise to avoid escalating it to a bigger fight. His malice made me doubt myself and see myself as weak, indecisive, and incapable of dealing with a bad situation.

I couldn't wait to run. I didn't like people who snapped for things like this, but I thought it was my problem, being too intolerant, too judgemental, too not "gentle."

After the gong show, we didn't really hang out as much, but we did continue to message each other. I had my doubts, but he seemed okay over MSN and played things quite cool. We kept dragging along, and I thought we both knew it wasn't anything significant. He seemed to be okay with it.

I traveled a lot for work during that time. Though we dated on and off, it didn't seem to be problematic. Time flew by, and in the summer of 2008, he asked me for a favor. His apartment's lease was up, so he had to move out immediately but was too busy to go out and find a place during that month as he had a big campaign going on at work. He asked if he could crash at my place for two weeks until the campaign was done. He was very sincere, and the favor didn't seem unreasonable. I was empathetic as I lived in the big city, and I knew how difficult it was to find a place so I agreed. Again, I didn't think much into it as I'd been traveling, and he still seemed to be perfectly normal. He also offered to pay some rent, but I rejected as I thought he would only stay for two weeks.

By the end of October, it was the same excuse that he was busy with work, and by this time I was pretty sure that he wanted to delay moving out as long as possible so I would be forced to stay with him. I was already tired of him asking so many questions, such as…

"Why don't you want to get married?"

"Because I don't want to."

"Why?"

"Can you talk to my mom when I call her?"

"No, I don't think it's appropriate."

"Why?"

"What do you think I should change to be with you?"

"Nothing, you just be yourself, and if it works it works. If not, it's not right."

"Why?"

I forgot about most of these questions, but according to my journal, I was really drained. Up to this point we were both cool, and I didn't expect anything radical would happen. Some red flags weren't raised quite yet. However, he told me that he really liked me multiple times, so before another trip to Beijing in November, I had a talk with him.

"Hey, as you know, I am going to go to Beijing for business next week."

"Yes, I know. I will try to find a place as soon as possible."

"It's been more than three months, so I would like you to actually move out when I come home. You can return the key then."

"But I am busy. I am sorry if you are upset. I will try." He seemed sincere.

"This is getting a little bit ridiculous. What if I didn't have a place, or there wasn't anyone else who could help? What were you going to do?"

"But you have a place!" He was humbly begging me.

"Yes, but that doesn't mean you can stay at my place."

"Your place? I thought we lived together."

I was shocked. "I have told you I want to stay at my place, alone."

"But we are dating, why waste money to rent another place? We are together anyways."

"Okay," I was getting really irritated. "Even though we are dating, I want to have my own space. I am not ready to move in with anyone, so please move out." I was so frustrated that I couldn't communicate with him smoothly. It felt like the four gray walls were pressing in toward me, and I was so upset that I stopped talking. I didn't want to accelerate the fight.

"Okay, don't be upset. I will find a place and move out by the time you are back."

I thought it was solved. He acted normal while I was in Beijing texting me he would move out soon. I didn't care much and just wanted this to end reasonably and peacefully.

After I got home, he didn't move out. I was so frustrated and furious, but I wanted to solve it peacefully like an adult. He stalled for another week and didn't seem to look around at all for a new place. On the 28th of November, I asked him to talk.

"I thought we talked about it…Menoetius, no matter how we get along or where this is going, I want you to move out. I need my own space." I was calm but really cold.

"I know, but I couldn't find a place." He looked at me with his beautiful eyes which I now just felt averse to.

"This is a big city. I am sure you can find a place."

"Okay, honestly, I want to marry you." He gave me a sly grin.

"What the hell! Which part didn't you understand? I don't want to get married. I want to live in my place, alone." He just pushed my biggest button.

"Think about it! We are together and already live together. Why toss and turn? Since we will keep seeing each other, why don't we just keep it the way it is?"

"Because I don't want to marry you, because I don't think we are compatible. Since you mentioned it, I don't really want to keep things the way they are either. I don't think we should keep seeing each other."

"Now you are telling me we are not compatible?" He turned pretty surly.

"What's the problem?"

Really, what was the problem? Wasn't this the most legitimate reason for people not being together?

"We've spent so much time together! And you are only telling me now?"

"We've known each other for just more than a year, and learning about a person takes time. After all this time we spent together, I realized that you are not right for me." I was on the verge of collapse. Just like every other time when we were communicating, we were not on the same channel, ever.

"No, it's an excuse. You are responsible for me."

Was I hearing this right? Responsible for what? Was he pregnant or something?

"People being attracted to each other doesn't mean that they get along fine. I don't want to settle down. I don't want to get married. I don't want to live with anybody. Is that clear?"

"Fuck you. You know what? I've been playing along for all this time. I've had enough. You are belittling me because I am from a small village. I am not good enough for you. I know you fucking despise me. You didn't even get angry with me until now because you think I am not worth it. You never even bother to argue with me. I've worked so hard to try to catch up, but you still look down on me," he yelled at me. "Since you don't care I am gonna screw you over. I am staying. I am not going anywhere." He snapped just like that.

I should have seen this coming. I should have known better. I should have been stronger. I was overwhelmed by the self-blaming and shame. How did I get to this point? Why did I even associate with this ugly person? What was my way out? My head was spinning.

"Watch your mouth! You know this is not true. I was talking about us not being compatible. I don't want to keep repeating myself. No matter what, please move out. This is my place."

"I am not leaving. There is no way you can ditch me like this. What can you do?"

What could I do? I didn't know. At a point I thought the only way to end it was to end myself. I had nowhere to go. It had been a headache that I could never talk him into leaving, but now it was a nightmare. I had never met anybody else like this. I had met arrogant people, short-tempered people, street kids even, but I felt powerless with this situation.

I started crying. He kept cursing me, "Tell you what, men with bare feet don't fear those with shoes. I have nothing to lose!"

"Why did you have to make this so ugly? Can't we just break up? We've already been to this point. How can we ever go back and be happy together?"

"Don't imagine you can get rid of me like garbage. No way! You people from good families have always been exploiting people like us."

"You act like garbage."

"Say that again. You look down on me?" He stared at me with fire in his eyes.

"You don't respect yourself. Look at what you are doing here. Shameless."

He pushed me and choked me against my closet as I mumbled, "Don't push me."

I was trying to fight, but he pinned me down to the closet board. I forget how long he kept me like that, but I remember I wasn't scared. Oddly, I was relieved. My mind was never clearer. *This is the end*, I told myself.

Maybe my calmness seemed creepy to him because he let go of me and started to slap himself. I looked at him emotionlessly. He then walked out of my place, foul-mouthed. I turned around looking at myself in the mirror. There were bruises and scars on my neck, wrist, and lower back.

I called a close friend and explained briefly what happened and then packed some basic stuff and went to stay at their place. I also took pictures of all the bruises and scars when I got there. Then I went to the police office first thing in the morning to file a report, but they said since we knew each other it's really hard for them to get involved. I was startled but couldn't say anything. My friend Tina came over right after she heard about and insisted to follow me closely just in case. When she heard this, she was so upset and said, "Will you only get involved if someone dies?"

"Hey, young lady, watch your words." No police wanted to help me.

We went back to the office. I was still working as that was the only thing keeping me sane. Tina didn't let me go anywhere without her. Soon Menoetius found out I had left. He started to call me every five minutes. I was literally shaking and almost felt like I had to pick up to stop it.

"Don't pick up." Tina was assertive. "Ask him to send messages to you just in case."

I totally agreed. I texted him to text me.

-Come back! I need to talk to you.

-*We are done talking. You leave with all your stuff, that's it.*

-I told you I didn't find a place to stay.

-*It's none of my business. You are an adult.*

-I need to talk to you.

-*I don't. Pack your stuff, leave.*

-I want you back.

-*We are done. Pack your stuff, leave.*

-Don't push me! I told you don't f*cking push me.

He came to my office and insisted on seeing me. Tina and I went downstairs. He told Tina to get out as he wanted to talk to me alone.

"Tina is not going anywhere. I am done talking to you. Like I said, pack your stuff, leave. Before that we have nothing to talk about."

"You think you are superior to me? Huh? Tina, you f*cking stay out of this," He spluttered.

"Or what?"

"I know where you work. This is not over!"

"Did you need my home address? Loser." Tina was so fearless and took the same aggressive momentum, which I couldn't really pull off. I always wanted to solve the problem properly, but in retrospect, there was no problem to solve. He was wrong.

He left so pissed off. When I later went back home to get some clothes while he wasn't there, I found he had changed my lock.

-If you want the key, come back home and let's talk. I have your journal as well. I finally know you didn't like me, you were just playing with me.

-Please return the key and my journal, it's private. Pack your stuff and leave.

-Still taking the high road? Let me see what you got. I know you look down on me. I don't care anymore. I go down, you go down.

-Listen to yourself. Don't be crazy.

-This is the last time I ask you to come home, or else I will burn down your house.

I was so worried not only because my place was in a historic building but because my neighbors were mostly seniors. What if they got hurt? I was so close to giving up and going back home.

"Don't go. Let him burn. I would have so much respect if he really did. He is just a coward. Trust me. People who make threats like this won't have the guts to do it." Tina was quite confident. She had all the toughness I needed then. "This is Shanghai, your building is a registered historical building. I will lend him ten guts to see if he dares to even touch it." She doubted he would actually do it.

I was desperate. Five days passed, and I couldn't handle it anymore. All I was thinking was that I couldn't end it without ending myself, but how sad would my dad be? I couldn't do that to him. He would be devastated. I couldn't do that to him. I called him and tried to tell him in a plain tone about what was happening, but I was shaking.

    He flew to Shanghai the next morning. I moved out from my friend's place, and we moved to a hotel. I didn't cry, but I felt humiliated, embarrassed, and ashamed. I couldn't forgive myself for letting my dad and friends worry so much, for not handling it better, for being weak and vulnerable, or for trapping myself in this kind of mud.

    My dad always stayed around except when I was at work. He accompanied me to work and would wait to pick me up after work. Even when I went to my friend's wedding as a bridesmaid, he waited in the hotel lobby. He insisted that I resign from my job and go back home with him.

    "I can't take the risk. He has hurt you and could hurt you again. He is crazy, so you can't rationalize with him. You can only avoid him." I could tell how concerned he was. He never asked me to do anything but to resign immediately, knowing how much I loved Shanghai. "I am just very worried about your safety. Please come home, even temporarily."

    Menoetius kept harassing me by text.

-I know you are looking for help. I don't care. Don't even think I would give up. Come back, then it's over. Or else, we will go down together. I won't let you live comfortably.

-Don't you like talking? Let's talk. You people from big cities are so snobbish. I am telling you we have dignity as well.

    I then remembered that I had his brother's phone number, and he mentioned that his mom came to Shanghai to take care of his brother's newborn baby. His brother and I had met once, and he seemed to be reasonable. I called him.

    "Hi, Xiao Yong, it's me."

"Oh, hello." He sounded surprised.

"I am not sure if you know what is going on with me and Menoetius."

"Oh, what's up?" He didn't know. This could be a tipping point.

"So we've fallen out with each other." I paused to find out if he really knew nothing about it.

"Oh, sorry about that. Everything alright?" I was assured he did not know.

"No, not really. He didn't take it well. He actually threatened to burn down my house. I have text records."

He gasped but didn't say anything.

"I really hope you or auntie can talk to him about it. He is now chasing a dead end, and I couldn't reason with him. Our breakup is between the two of us, but his committing a crime is not. Not to mention I live in a historical building, and my neighbors are grandpas and grandmas. If he burns down the house, and they can't get out, what happens? Would you or auntie really want to visit him in jail? What would that cause for your whole family? Is that really worthwhile? For a breakup?"

"I understand. Thanks for telling me. Let me take care of it."

Later that day, Menoetius texted me again.

-How dare you! Why did you involve my family?
-*Think about them next time before you do anything.*
-It will never end.

I didn't know the end was coming.

My boss heard about the story when I resigned. He offered to help, but I just didn't want to get more people involved. He was kind enough to agree that I could work remotely when I was away. My dad went to talk to his friend in prosecution in

Shanghai while my mom was also talking to her friends to find a solution.

Suddenly it all came to a halt. I received a package on the December 7 with the key to the new lock on my door and my journal. Maybe it was my call with his brother, maybe Tina called him, or maybe someone had done something. It all stopped so abruptly. I had no clue at all and no intention to find out. Some unanswered questions didn't need to be answered.

I went back to my place with Tina and my dad. All my clothes were dragged out from my closet and tossed on the floor and so were my shoes. It was a mess. I couldn't stop weeping. My home was ruined—my safe bubble, my private space, my life in Shanghai. I moved to a temporary rental place and reluctantly went back to my hometown in early January 2009. It was the only thing I could do to compensate how much I made my dad worry about me.

I lost thirteen pounds in ten days.

I cried.

I regretted.

I blamed myself.

I was ashamed that it happened to me.

I had been through so much humiliation and fear.

I felt violated because he manipulated me by using my politeness, sympathy, decency, and "weakness" against me.

It could have been worse, and I was blessed.

It's okay because I wasn't defeated. It's okay because I finally ended it. It's okay because I became more aware of myself. It was like Nirvana for me that I was able to go back to Shanghai no longer blaming myself and without fear.

What mattered the most was that even at the worst point, I didn't give up on my true self. I didn't compromise by agreeing to marry him. I chose to stay reasonable and to not seek revenge. I didn't let my politeness, sympathy, and decency get destroyed. I kept thinking that what happened could be a consequence but could also be a cause, as Buddhism indicates. I kept praying for him to let go of his obsessiveness and for me to let go of my hatred.

It's painful, but why did I write this story down? It really wouldn't be a complete story until I wrote down. Being complete is part of how I let go and move on.

If you are reading this and related to these horrible things or had something even more disturbing happen to you, please remember: you are not alone. Global estimates published by the World Health Organization indicate that "about one in three (35 percent) of women worldwide have experienced either physical and/or sexual intimate partner violence or non-partner sexual violence in their lifetime. Most of this violence is intimate partner violence. Worldwide, almost one-third (30 percent) of women who have been in a relationship report that they have experienced some form of physical and/or sexual violence by their intimate partner in their lifetime."

"Calls to helplines have increased five-fold in some countries as rates of reported intimate partner violence increase because of the COVID-19 pandemic. Restricted movement, social isolation, and economic insecurity are increasing women's vulnerability to violence in the home around the world." (Ending Violence Against Women, UN Women.)

It's never an ideal situation, but it's not a dead end either.

You can always leave. I could, and you can as well.

You are strong enough to take care of yourself. I was, and you are as well.

You always have a choice. Always.

CHAPTER 6

A TALE OF FIVE CITIES—NEW YORK

I should have been excited, happy, and full of hope, but I was not—not even close.

It was the night before I left Shanghai for New York in 2014. My friends threw a farewell party for me, and we went to karaoke. I picked "Empire State of Mind" by Jay-Z and Alicia Keys. It was such a great tune, but I got choked with sobs. I loved *Sex and the City*, and I had always longed to live in New York City, with a career, a bunch of good friends, and a lot of shows and exhibitions.

It was more like a journey of the unknown.

When the relationship with XM became more and more uncertain after I moved to Shanghai, I was desperate for a change but still not ready to move on. After a really bad breakup with the guy who hit me, I went back to Kunming for a break. We met up from time to time when I was in Kunming in 2009, but our relationship turned so bitter that I wasn't enjoying any of it anymore. By my birthday in April, we were almost trying too hard to keep up with it.

"What would you like for your birthday? It's the first time we celebrate your birthday together." XM asked.

"Nothing else, just spending it together."

"Of course I will spend it with you, but what would you like for a gift?"

"I can't think of any. It's up to you. I just want to be with you."

"Okay, let me think about it."

He left for a business trip the day before my birthday and told me he would be back by dinner on my birthday.

He did not come back.

He did not call or text.

I didn't feel much this time. I thought I probably didn't love him anymore. We'd burned up whatever we had, and he didn't bother to save it. So instead of spending it with him, I spent my birthday with a group of friends.

He called me the next morning. "I was so busy yesterday."

"So busy that you didn't even go to the toilet?" He might have been pissed, but I couldn't care less.

I started to dislike who I was when I was around him. I didn't want to be bitter or mean. I didn't want to be complaining, and I didn't want to be always waiting.

After two months, I moved back to Shanghai. By the end of 2009, I got my dream job, moved to a new place, started to learn French, and resumed dancing. I started over. I admitted to myself that XM and I were over. I could not bring myself to stay in Kunming just to be around him. I wanted to live in Shanghai, live my own life.

Between 2009 and 2011, I had one missed call from him. I deleted his contact in my phone, but of course I still could recognize his number. I didn't call back, mainly because I didn't know what to say. He called me again around the summer, and this time I picked up.

"Ya'ya, do you have a business trip to Beijing soon?" He didn't sound right.

"No I don't. What's up? How are you doing?"

"Not very good. I am having a gout attack. Really bad…I am just in so much pain. I can't move at all." His voice was low and lifeless—so very different from how he used to be. I was shocked.

"That's really bad. Is someone taking care of you now?"

I knew from my family members that there wasn't any treatment for gout, so when there was an attack, one just had to endure as long as it went on. I wasn't sure what I could help with.

"Yes my sister and niece. If you happen to come to Beijing, I would love to see you. I am just in so much pain, and I wanted to just see you." He never talked to me in this tone either, almost begging. I was even more surprised.

"Who knows when the next time will be?" He sighed.

It didn't sound right. There was more to his low spirit than the gout. I knew he was active. He liked hiking in the mountains and walking around. Maybe the immobility was really disheartening him. Maybe he took it as the sign of getting old which could be really difficult for him to swallow.

"I will fly over tomorrow," I said.

I didn't need a business trip to go to see him. I loved him, and I had never seen or heard him like this. For the sake of seeing him for the last time if somewhere were to go really wrong, I wanted to go and see him. I wanted to live with no regret, and I didn't want things get to a point where it was too late to avoid regret.

I took a week off and flew to Beijing.

His niece picked me up at the airport. It was the first time we met, and she was my age, super nice and authentic. I was wondering if she knew about us or exactly how much he told her about this trip. She seemed to be quite cool, and we were very normal on the way back to his house, chitchatting quite well as we both worked for advertising agencies. I had never been to his new house since he had bought it recently. She dropped me off in front of the front door and went to park. "The door is open," she quickly mentioned. I pushed the door open. The foyer wasn't long, and there was a long couch facing the front door. He was sitting there waiting for me, looking feckless.

"You're here," he greeted me. His voice was older than I remembered, and his hair was more gray.

"Hi."

I couldn't say much more. I was quite emotional. It was the first time I had a strong sense of the age gap between us in such a vivid, almost crucial, way.

During my week there, he didn't spend a lot of time talking to me. Instead he was working in his study. I went to see a few friends but just stayed around most of the time. One day we were having watermelon on the porch, and his older brother dropped by. He was a bit surprised to see me.

"You came as well?" He was still very intimidating, authoritative, and brief.

"Yes, I am here for a week."

The last time I met his brother was when XM and I first broke up when I was still in Beijing. He called me out of nowhere and wanted to meet up with me. He was basically telling me if XM was acting odd in our relationship, then I should try to understand and tolerate it. He later told me that XM had one wrong button to push, and it was the topic of relationships. No one could talk to him about "settling down." It was very conventional for his peers to get married and have children early in their life, yet he was still single with no kids. The subject was taboo for him, and he would just shut down whenever his family tried to persuade him to find a partner, his brother told me.

I didn't know why. Maybe he was hurt before. Whatever may have happened in his past, I knew the result. XM once told me he was never going to get married. Honestly, I was quite relieved as I didn't want to get married either. So the family stopped talking about it. That's why his brother went through the trouble of seeing me, as I was the first woman XM had ever brought to introduce to the family since he moved back to China. He thought things may have been serious between us. He didn't want to intrude in our matters, but if we were just fighting about small things then he'd hoped we would stay together. I had to admit that conversation pushed me to get back together with him.

"Good." He nodded and walked away, and XM followed him hobbling.

In front of his big brother, XM was like the most humble boy waiting to be disciplined—a very different and rare side of him. One could easily tell that he looked up to his big brother very much.

He wasn't as bad as he sounded in the call, so I was relieved and ready to leave. The night before I returned to Shanghai, he talked to me about moving back to New York. I was listening but genuinely didn't think it had anything to do with me.

"I was thinking about acquiring some tourism properties in the States. So I can spend half of the year there. A good half—April to October."

"What about your business in Kunming?"

"It's passed the development phase and entered into a retaining phase, so it's okay for me to leave from time to time."

"Oh, okay."

"I was thinking about getting this house upstate as a hub to connect all the properties. So we can stay and work there." He was showing me a place on his computer. "I will need someone to be there to manage the business. All the properties have existing management teams, so I just need someone to represent me when I am not there. You said you liked New York, didn't you?"

"Yes."

"Do you want to come?"

"To work there?"

"To work, to stay, depends on what you want." Typical, he was still very ambiguous about his agenda.

"I don't think it depends on what I want. Maybe you can let me know when everything is more in place?"

Where would this go? Would I get into another tangled interaction with him? I worked so hard to get out of it. Was I ready to jump in again? I was tired of his ambiguity, his lack of commitment, his dominance in our previous relationship. Was I in the right place to try it again? Most importantly, would I go back to being his employee, his girlfriend, or what?

I had one answer certain though: he would never answer any of those questions. I was always "figuring it out." I didn't even feel safe enough to talk about them with him. It was like being in dark water, with only a shed of light coming through. I could see it but didn't know where it came from, how far it was, or whether it was relevant.

I had my own assurance that he wasn't dying, and it wasn't our last meeting, so I returned to Shanghai as planned.

We stayed in touch, but I didn't get many updates until 2014. We met up again, and he told me all of the transactions were complete for the tourism properties and the house and that he was thinking about going in April. He once again suggested that I go with him. I would only work half of the year and the rest of time I could stay in the city or travel back.

If all it took to start a life in New York, the city I've been longing for, was to believe in him, I would take the chance. If all it took to find an answer to our relationship was to believe in him, I would take this chance.

Yes, I was moving further from my family and friends. Yes, I left a developing career behind. Yes, there was so much uncertainty in this plan. I cried hard the night before as I sang the song at karaoke with my friends.

I flew to New York in the middle of April 2014.

We toured around the properties across the upper state and stayed in the house in Utica at the beginning. It used to be a castle on the top of the hill, but the stable part was sold separately many years ago, so the property only had the main house with driveways, gardens, and a backyard. I liked the house because of its characteristic heritage. It was a vast neighborhood as the houses were quite spread out.

One day when we got home, there were many cars parked around the neighborhood, very unusually, and even two on our driveway. I was curious.

"Why are there so many cars?"

"Oh the neighbor across the street is having a party tonight and asked me if they can park as there is an overflow."

"I see. How come we are not invited?" I was kidding. I didn't expect to be invited. We've never met the neighbors, so why would they invite us? Parking on our empty driveway was a small favor that only cost a "thank you."

"We were."

"Okay…?" He had not told me anything about a potential party.

"I rejected. I don't see why we need to go to some party with strangers."

"But we have no social life at all."

"Why do you need a social life?"

"To get to know people around?"

"I don't see any fun in going. Just stay in."

I was disappointed. I wasn't a party animal and, to be fair, could never be one in the middle of nowhere, but I didn't mind having some fun or a distraction once in a while. I was not naive in wanting to live a life like what I saw in *Sex and the City*. I knew that was just a show, but I needed friends; I needed to talk to people; I needed more in my life rather than just work and him. That evening, I stayed at home and watched some TV show, while he worked in the study alone. We barely talked. We were not really compatible in terms of social needs.

What really irritated me and emphasized the fact that we were not compatible was an incident that occurred later on. We had never lived together and had only spent time in hotels and resorts back when we were dating, so I didn't have an idea about his style in his day-to-day life.

His gout was still lingering, but he could drive and walk slowly. One day, when we went grocery shopping, he was getting ribs, and I was trying to get vegetables. He picked on me about my choice, but I was so checked out because I didn't even want to argue with him. When we got back home, he started to make broth.

"I thought you had gout, you shouldn't be having broth."

He ignored me and went ahead. As I expected, his gout got worse and intolerable again.

"We should really stop having broth. Can I make you something else? Like salad?"

"I got the ribs so you can have some meat! It was for you."

"I am fine being vegetarian." I didn't even know why he blamed me for it.

Later that week when our trash can was full, I was going to take the trash out.

"Hang on, let's get the car." I didn't know why, but I took the garbage and got ready.

He drove to a place like a town center where there were a bunch of commercial properties, restaurants, and gas stations. He stopped at the back of a line of shops, right in front of the commercial dumpster, which was almost as tall as I was.

"Go dump it now."

"What?" I was stunned.

"Go, hurry up, now!"

I grabbed the garbage bag and got out of the car. He stayed in the car just watching me, offering no help, keeping the engine running like a getaway car. If someone came, would he just drive away? I sneaked up to the big dumpster, opened the lid with difficulty, and threw the bag in. That was one of most humiliating moments in my life. Just because nobody was watching didn't mean that it was okay.

He was still pushing me, telling me to "hurry up!" I went back to the car and couldn't say a word. He explained that because he didn't come back until recently, he hadn't paid for the trash pickup service yet. The previous owner of the house lived in the area and helped check in from time to time. This could be easily arranged. It was just so unnecessary on so many levels.

Eventually, we got to a frozen point. I stopped talking to him except when it concerned work. Surely I was pretty cold and defensive, but I couldn't act normal any longer. I was very irritated and secretly blamed him for bringing me to this point. Looking back, I learned not to blame other people for the situation, no matter what. That can only lead to a narrow mind and hatred. It never helps any situation.

A few weeks later, we came back to New York City to meet with business partners and showed them the properties. I stayed supportive and useful. After meeting with two groups of people, XM and I still hadn't talked about my compensation or terms or my role—in the business and in his life.

I had enough. I didn't care about potential business opportunities or a personal relationship with him. It just didn't work, him and me. Maybe he was stimulated by my indifference because he started to provoke me more and more. He belittled me so much to a point where I asked him one day, "Is there anything good about me in your mind?"

"Of course!"

"What is it? I really need to know because it seems to you I don't have a single redeeming feature. All you talk about is my flaws."

"I won't tell you or else you will be too proud."

I became more and more irritated. I'd never been so sick of him. Without knowing how powerful the feeling of resentment could be, I unconsciously started to pray for him to disappear from my life.

When we got back to the city again, he told me we were going to meet up with his partners from the law firm that night, the group I met in Shanghai back in 2006. It had been eight years, and we were still in an awkward situation, in my opinion at least. I didn't want to meet them without any clarification. So I decided to talk to him.

"XM," this was the first time I called him by name in ten years. "I want to talk to you."

He lit a cigarette and was listening.

"It's not clear to me where this is going. It is different from what we've talked about before I came."

"It will only happen when you make it happen," he said. While he was right, it was the wrong time to preach me. I was so tired of his rhetoric.

"I've given some thought to it. I am going back to Shanghai. If you want me to help you with the business, let's talk about the package. If you want to stay in a relationship, please also tell me explicitly. Either way, I need time to think about it, and I'd prefer to go back home while doing that." I was unprecedentedly relieved.

"What are you talking about? You wanted to come to New York. I brought you here. What more do you want? You've never talked to me about your thoughts and always kept to yourself. How can I know what you want?"

I wanted respect. "Thank you very much for this opportunity. I have told you what I want. I also want to know what you really want and see if it's what I want. Before we figure that out, I want to go home."

"If you leave, I won't bring you back again, and it's not my fault. You need to tell your dad it's your decision."

How could someone I used to love so much become so hideous? What was he afraid of?

I didn't even know where to start. "It's not about whose fault it is, and my dad supports my decisions. I am simply telling you my thoughts. I also wanted to know yours. Before we clear things up, I am not going back upstate next week, and I don't see the point of joining you at the dinner tonight either. I will stay in the city for a while to look around, and I have a few former colleagues that I wanted to meet. I hope you can understand."

He was smoking silently, taking a long pause. The silence was smothering, and I stepped out of the apartment.

The next day, I received a message from him telling me he went back to upstate. I was still staying at his apartment in the Upper West Side and didn't hear from him until a week later. He sent me a picture of his SUV crashed.

-I had a car accident that night going up north.

-*OMG, what happened?*

-I don't know, was just absentminded. Before I realized, I had hit the fence on the highway, going 70 miles an hour.

-*ARE YOU OKAY?*

-Yes, I was fine. The air bag didn't come out, so my nose was fine and I didn't get hurt.

I gasped, and suddenly the fear crept up my spine. There was only one moment I hated someone so much that I wished he would disappear completely. That was then and him, but I never truly wanted to hurt him. The relationship didn't work, but it's never a reason to hurt anyone. How did I become so resentful, because I was with someone that I didn't agree with? The dynamic between us had become so twisted that it triggered a very dark side in my heart. It was not right, and, most importantly, it was not good for me.

It wasn't even who I really was. Before him, I never had such thoughts about another person. I believed intention mattered the most as advocated in Buddhism. Cursing others was a burden of sin and would lead to bad karma. I didn't want to be devoured by my own negative intentions. I didn't want to pay a debt if something bad really happened to him. I couldn't afford to live in regret for the rest of my life. I had to leave him for good this time, as if we hadn't hurt each other enough last time.

He was clearly hit hard, probably more mentally. I could imagine a few reasons, but after all, he would never tell me. Maybe what hit him the most was that no one had really "rejected" him like that, especially when he "offered" something. His expectation was probably that I would be over the moon to receive whatever was thrown at me. Another reason I could think of was the fact that I had changed. I had grown up from a young girl to a woman, and he probably felt he had lost control. I knew better about what I did and did not want for my life, yet he may have had different opinions. Also, I realized we were not compatible, while the definition of compatibility was probably not in his dictionary. Regardless, there should not be any resentment.

For ten years, he raised me up to the peak of my affection but also dragged me down to the chasm of my oppression.

If I had any remnant of hope, by now it had vanished into thin air.

This was the end.

CHAPTER 7

A TALE OF FIVE CITIES—VANCOUVER

It was January 6, 2017.

It was the day of double epiphanies. According to Marriam-Webster, the first is defined as the Canadian holiday of "January 6 observed as a church festival in commemoration of the coming of the Magi as the first manifestation of Christ to the Gentiles or in the Eastern Church in commemoration of the baptism of Christ." The second being my own "sudden manifestation or perception of the essential nature or meaning of something or an illuminating discovery, realization, or disclosure."

On this day, I brought final closure to a meaningful past with XM.

When XM first learned that I would move to Canada, he dissed the decision. "Why would you even go there? It's so cold."

"I am going to Vancouver. It's not that bad."

Besides, it was my decision. Why was he challenging it even before asking me why? Why didn't he even bother to first listen to what I wanted? Why was he so judgmental? Why didn't he show any interest in knowing the details? But once again, I internalized these questions and didn't ask any of them out loud. It was my pattern with him. I usually swallowed half of my real opinion because I didn't like conflict, disagreement, or arguing. Gradually, I learned that it wasn't conflict to simply have different thoughts on a subject. I didn't have to convince anyone, but I shouldn't have to conceal my thoughts either.

Shortly after I returned to Shanghai from New York in 2014, my immigration process to Canada suddenly moved forward. I didn't want to leave Shanghai again, but I didn't stop the process either. Looking back, there is no harm in giving ourselves as many choices as possible within our capability. By September 2015, I hit a really bad depression. It was not diagnosed, but it was so bad that for about a week I just wanted to jump out of the window of the fifteenth floor every time I went back home.

My mental health wasn't the only thing going wrong in my life then. Career-wise, I was working for a start-up company as well as other freelance projects. It was referred to me by a close friend, and things started out well. I developed the business and launched the project in two new cities successfully. However, I was traveling so often that I was fatigued both physically and mentally, and I was also busy building local teams to run the project properly. It was a steep learning curve but helpful for my career development, so I had nothing to complain about.

However, by the end of the project, the COO of the company decided to implement a cash penalty for under-delivery of my whole team in one of the cities. I explained that we didn't miss too much of the KPIs (key performance indicators).

Plus, I'd talked with him about lowering the KPI, as the market needed longer to catch up prior to the appraisal. Back then, he didn't provide any definitive feedback. I couldn't help but wonder it might be his technique to drag it out and see. Regardless, I offered to cut my bonus but not my team's because their base wasn't much. The COO rejected it with a hard no. I later learned it might have had to do with financial difficulties due to the valuation adjustment mechanism of the C-round fundraising. But I was never clearly communicated with, and, in retrospect, my success of launching in these two new cities was actually what closed the deal. It proved our business model scalable. I felt so bad for myself but more for my team. I also blamed myself for not being tough enough to fight for them.

Personal lifewise, I was dating a friend then, and he had always been super supportive and understanding. One day in the summer when I finally came back from a business trip, we met up as usual. I was exhausted, and when we were having drinks, he told me that he fell in love with a girl who just joined his company. I understood but asked him if we could talk about it later as I was really tired and annoyed with my work; I wanted to keep something in place in my life. He couldn't wait to clear things up with me so he could have a clean start to date this girl.

I messed up. Of course I was not going to restrict him, and I respected him very much. But I was more so sad because the one thing predictable in my life—that one person who would always be there—had just changed without any heads-up. Looking back, I didn't date him because I loved him; I dated him because he was always available for me. There was always going to be a point when he would make his decision to end this not-so-healthy relationship, which was fine. I just wished it wasn't that exact moment. Of course I learned the hard way that I would never date someone I didn't romantically like ever again. But back then, that deepened my sense of powerlessness.

The lowest point came when I learned the news that my college ex-boyfriend was going to get married with my ex-bestie. (LIKE, WHAT WAS THAT?) That's fine…we broke up a hundred years ago. The news was delivered by my friend Edward. Edward told me more as gossip because he wasn't expecting that I was experiencing such a bad depression. He learned it from a friend of my ex's, who jokingly told Edward about the connection among us three and joked that I was the loser that was still in love with my ex-boyfriend. I didn't even know him personally. How did he get that impression? I was so irritated. Why couldn't they just leave me alone and live happily ever after?

Then I did start to feel like a loser. Everything seemed to be falling apart simultaneously, and I had absolutely no capacity to notice anything positive in my life. Everything flopped because of me. I wasn't good enough. I could have handled it better. If only I had done something differently, if only I had not done something, if only I wasn't existing…would all these questions be answered? Would all these problems go away? Would this world be a better place just without me?

By the end of that Saturday, I was in a horrible situation. I stayed up very late after dinner with Edward. Ben, a close friend who let me stay with him, always went to bed late, and he stayed awake with me that night. Seeing that I couldn't stop crying, he showed me a music video by Mika Nakashima for one of her most famous songs, 僕が死のうと思ったのは ("I've Thought about Going to Die"). I knew he was concerned and that he knew I wasn't in the right place because he had other friends stuck in depression. He later told me if I wasn't any better by Sunday, he would take me to the hospital.

I sobbed harder after watching the music video. It touched me so deeply on so many levels. It started with a lot of devastating feelings of hopelessness. There were a couple of situations that resonated with me deeply, such as the disappointment towards myself. Then from the very bottom of desperation, toward the end, the song presented that there could be hope because some people show up in our lives and make us like the world a little more. That reminded me of all the people I valued in my life, those who made me like this world.

I started to imagine their reactions toward the news of my death. Do I really want to create this pain for them? Do I not honor my love and care for them? As long as I kept going, there would be hope. I then started to regain my consciousness, thoughts, and connection to my true self.

We watched it a couple of times, and I calmed down a little. Ben said, "You know, the relationship between people is fluid, so is it between people and matters." I told him I wanted to think about it, and I was fine to be alone. He went to bed.

But I still couldn't fall asleep after Ben said goodnight. I smoked three packs of cigarette throughout the night. I couldn't get out of the bed on Sunday until three in the afternoon.

Triston, another friend, came by and said he hadn't had lunch yet and asked me to grab pho with him so he didn't have to be alone. I felt slightly needed and went out with him. The broth was warm and tasty, and the pho was easy to swallow and comforting. We didn't really talk about me. He was just there, chitchatting, making me feel there was still something normal in my life.

Later on, Edward asked me to join him for dinner at his place. We hung out a lot usually, but he probably heard from Ben that day about my situation. We lived close by, so I walked over. On my walk over, I felt like I was floating, and the world around me seemed blurry. He made me dinner, and we chatted.

"Have you ever thought that maybe it's not about you, about what you have done or haven't done; things would be the way they are anyways. You are a bit obsessed with the idea of you having control over everything in your life. Step back and detach a little."

He knew me too well. It was what I needed to hear at that time. I couldn't see through the mist because I was too swamped. Hearing something from a fresh perspective was very helpful for me to disengage from the entanglement.

I was grateful that I was staying with Ben, as well as his cat, Bo Li, and dog, Le Le. I was grateful that I was surrounded by friends who really cared for me and understood me. I was grateful that I had a choice. It probably would not be the case for everyone, but I humbly ask anyone to find even the faintest glimmers of light.

I couldn't think of any other way to shake things up other than start a new life all over again. I decided to go with the landing process of my immigration to Canada. If there was only one person who could yank me out of my situation, it was myself. I had to make the change.

Speaking of which, it happened also by coincidence. When I started to learn French back in 2010, I met a classmate working at an immigration agency. He was studying French in order to immigrate to Québec, Canada. After he knew that my brother's family lived in Vancouver, he suggested that I could apply just to have an option. He needed cases for his performance. "Besides, you don't need to pay until you are successful," he said. So I applied, and according to him, the process would take about 9–12 months. We both were waiting for the result since then. It was a bit random, but I couldn't stop thinking how all these random decisions lead us to our destiny.

Five years passed, and neither of us heard back anything. He even left the agency and handed me over to another case manager. I received a call from her when I was in New York asking if I wanted to switch my application from the Québec program to the federal program as the new job vacancy matched with my experience. I agreed but didn't expect much as it usually took longer to apply for the federal program. She told me it would take more than twenty-four months. It was the summer of 2014. By the summer of 2015, she was surprised that my case had been expedited, so much that I was required to have health exam already. When I asked her about how much longer it would be, she no longer had an idea. "I've never seen the federal case move so fast. Maybe another six months?" The next thing we knew, my permanent residence was issued in October 2015.

With everything going on and my landing window to immigrate expiring in six months, I decided to at least complete the process.

My brother's family lives in Metro Vancouver, so landing in Vancouver made most of the sense, not to mention that Vancouver has always been famous for its beautiful weather and nature. I had no idea what I was going to face before arriving in Vancouver in January 2016. I had never been to Canada, but I thought the proper challenge of starting in a new place could help me detach from my depression. That was also based on my awareness of who I was, how I respond to situations, and why I wanted it.

I can never forget the day I arrived in Vancouver. It took four hours to finally get through my immigration process at customs while my brother was waiting for me outside in his car. Thank goodness there was Wi-Fi in the terminal. My brother kept checking with me how the process was going, and my sister-in-law asked me a few times if we were on the way back home yet as my niece couldn't wait to see me.

Life couldn't feel more real in that moment.

When I finally stepped out the arrivals terminal, it was already dusk, and the sky was so clear and high. The sunset made the sky the color of macaron blue and pink which was the Pantone color of that year. I knew I made the right decision.

Meanwhile, XM and I hadn't stayed in much contact since. But coincidentally—or maybe miraculously—we had a call on the day of the Epiphany, 2017.

"How is Vancouver?" He sounded perfunctory.

"Good. How are you? Are you in New York or Kunming?"

"Kunming, it's too cold to be in New York now."

I didn't know how, but we started to talk about our last interaction in New York.

"You've never turned out to be the person I hoped you would be. I am very disappointed with you as you never achieved what I expected you to do. I gave you an opportunity, but you didn't grab it. There are not many chances like this in one's life."

I started to get really emotional and confused. Did I miss something? What opportunity was he talking about? Working in New York? I thought we had talked about it before I left—either him offering me a package or letting me know what he wanted from me. What was this complex of being my rescuer? What was this complex of there being nothing in it for him the entire time? Did he want me to owe him or something?

"What did you expect of me?" I was sobbing. I wasn't in the best place of my life either. I just started a new life and wasn't fully sure about what I was looking for either. So his words really got to me.

"Never mind now. You will never get to that level. I overestimated you."

I got the notion of tough love, but this was like too tough, no love. I started to cry harder. He could be right. Yes, I may have overestimated myself. Yes, I may never get to where I aspired myself to be. Yes, I may never be good enough. I did not have all the answers and probably never would. But I could still try my best to live a life that's meaningful to me, to enjoy the journey, and to reconcile with myself.

However, I still looked up to him as I thought he was one of the smartest people I had ever known. So I humbly asked, "What do you think I can improve?"

"You will never get there. It's no use to talk about it anymore…" as if I was a lost cause. But if somewhere could never be reached, would it still be a destination? This was when I finally knew that he never accepted me as who I was, even though he was attracted to who I was. He could not live with it.

"You were telling people on the phone that I didn't offer you a package, nor a solution. You were complaining that you were not fulfilled with the life there. I heard you on the phone. You don't appreciate how much I've done for you…"

If one felt they were doing too much for the other, one must have loved too little.

I was surprised how, word-by-word, he remembered what I said even three years later. It suddenly dawned on me that he didn't forget about anything, that he was still holding on to it. I had the epiphany that he was the one who couldn't talk himself into letting go. I grew up and moved on. It's fascinating how others could help us see ourselves more clearly. He could judge me all he wanted, but it was me who was living my life.

We couldn't have avoided crossing each other's paths in our lifetime. After all, what we encounter in our life could be predestined, but I can choose how I want to move forward emotionally.

CHAPTER 8

TIME ZONES

There is no such thing as being too early or too late. We are just in different time zones at our own pace.

I was almost late for my French class last night, rushing in when everyone was ready for *quoi de neuf* (what's up).

I started to study French as a hobby in 2010 at l'Alliance Française in Shanghai. After a full-steam-ahead three-year class every Saturday from 9 a.m. to 3 p.m., I loosened up and stopped when I moved to Vancouver in 2016. Then I found out about l'Alliance Française in Vancouver, so I decided to continue.

As it's the same organization, I was quite used to the setting. My first teacher here was a young Arab French lady. She was really nice and shy and never gave us homework. She wasn't strict about preparation or class participation, so I was quite slack. When the term finished, some people were dropping out, so I was assigned to a higher class for the coming term. The new teacher was a shriveled, fair lady with a serious face. Her name was Yvette. She wore a pair of dark-framed glasses and her blond, tight, curly hair was well shaped. If she had put on a black gown with hood, she'd be the mid-century governess in a castle that every kid was afraid of.

Different from my previous instructor, she ran her class very intensely and required our undivided attention. We always started the class with *quoi de neuf*, which I thought was routine, but she was very serious about it. She listened to everyone very carefully and made sure everyone spoke coherently even if it took a while. Then she would go through the homework questions one by one, asking us to read out loud whenever there was a paragraph or a sentence. The actual learning portion of the class didn't begin until the second half.

There were only five of us in the class. With *quoi de neuf* every week, we became quite familiar with each other. It's fascinating that a group of strangers knew such intimate details of each other's life.

I muddled through my last night as I didn't have much to talk about except work. Louise went last and her *quoi de neuf* was that her daughter was pregnant with the second baby.

"Oh, my daughter is just twenty years old, and she's having her second baby! It's just too fast. Too fast! And I have to take care of her baby. I want to help her since she is so young! I have to help her, but I am tired, and I don't even have my own life." Even in French, her words were like a runaway train with her hands in the air moving around.

The whole class was really surprised. Yvette asked, "How many kids do you have?"

"Three."

"When did you have them?"

"In my early twenties, one followed by the other." She seemed completely detached from the comment five seconds ago.

No wonder she looked so not like a grandma. She was from Italy originally. We had learned bits and pieces before that she was an interpreter and that she also taught hula dance. She had long, thick, dark coiled-up curly hair. Her body looked like a dancer's, full of life and energy. In my mind the most amazing thing about her were her eyes. They were the color of sapphire blue twinkling in a sudden bright light.

"I had children when I was so young. It was not easy, but my daughter…it's not easy!"

"It's great to have a baby when you were younger," Bonnie, who usually sat on my left-hand side commented. "When I was having my son, I was forty-one. Ugh, I felt like half of my life was gone. That was difficult!" I guessed that she must have been about sixty since she had previously shared she was retired. She was originally from Hong Kong.

She used to be a flight attendant for Air Canada all the way up until her retirement. She had seen the world. She was very fair, very slim, and very graceful. She always dressed up, typically with an earthen color cardigan and a pair of smoke pants. She wore loafers a lot, unobtrusive as well. One could appear very elegant after working on an aircraft for forty-something years. She was using an A5 size notebook with a pink cover and plastic coat. Her writing was very delicate. She studied very hard and had the best listening level in the class.

"When did you get married?" asked Yin. We usually sat in a U-shape, facing the teacher and the screen. Yin was sitting on the left end of the U.

Bonnie said, "Two months prior to my due date."

So strange what brings people together. One would never expect us to meet in our day-to-day lives, yet here we all were. One small, seemingly insignificant detail of our lives had brought us together. This has always fascinated me. Buddhism teaches us that people are preordained to meet. Our lives could be rivers crossing and flowing away in different directions, or we could merge and go on toward the ocean together.

"Did you get married because you were in love?" asked Yin, sounding genuinely innocent.

Yin was the second generation of a Taiwanese immigrant family. She studied biology and her *quoi de neuf* last night was being admitted as a full-time scientist by Vancouver General Hospital. She was a girl seemingly with no edge. Spotless round face with a pair of black-framed glasses, she didn't seem to pay much attention to her looks. Her hair was straight in pageboy style, and it didn't seem that she put a ton of effort into it. She dressed up without edge either—no outstanding color or style, just very humble. But in French class, she was the daring one, always challenging Yvette to wrap up the class early because she was tired and wanted to go home.

"Of course not," Bonnie blew the love fairy away right in front her edgeless face. "It was an accident. I just didn't reject the arrangement from the fate."

Yin immediately fell into the dilemma, a genuinely innocent dilemma. "How did you know the arrangement was right or not?" She had never been in a relationship.

"You don't!" Louise couldn't wait to jump in. "People just don't know! I've been divorced for fifteen years. With three children, I still chose to divorce because he wasn't right for me. He wasn't the right person." She was shaking her head lightly.

"Yes, you won't know until you make a choice," Bonnie chimed in with Louise.

"What do you think, Anne?" Yvette could tell Yin was not very satisfied with the answer. She called on the lady on Yin's right-hand side.

"You would know if it's the right one," Anne was quiet and sophisticated. She was Caucasian, and her short blond hair was nicely styled. She was tall, thin, and beautiful. Bonnie and Anne looked similar to me. She always wore the lipstick that you could tell was properly picked to match her scarf with very good taste. Her life rhythm was quite normal: two kids, both grown up and married. She retired with her spouse, and they were just enjoying their retired life.

Since everyone was quite heated about this topic, Yvette simply didn't start the new lesson. She called on David as well. He sat on my right-hand side and was the only male in the class. We'd love to know about his perspective.

"Oh, I don't have kids!" Everybody turned around and looked at him. David was a pilot working for Air Canada before he retired. Though his hair was silver, his body was totally straight when he was in class. His cheeks were ruddy, and he appeared very rigorous. He wasn't used to the fast pace of Yvette's class, but he was always jolly and smiling.

"My wife and I are very, very passionate about hiking. We decided that we didn't want to spend time on raising kids, so we don't have kids." He was cheerful and content as always.

They turned to me, expecting me to share. "As for me," I shared, "I don't have kids. I do believe in true love. I am still single, and I am still looking for true love. I agree with Louise, if it's not the right person it's never too late to get out of the relationship. I think that it is very hard to see if the person is right or if the arrangement is right before you get into, but I think I will always follow my heart. And I think as long as two people are on the same page, like David and his wife, then the relationship is good."

The five of us, literally from all over the world, meeting here with such different life experiences—it was almost like a miniature curio of life stages with each one having a sample selected. The only thing in common was that we lived our lives our own way. In a certain way, we were all quite lucky. Within such a small group, there were so many possibilities of life represented.

Is there a so-called bucket list for life? Is there a timeline for the listed items? What if we just missed the deadline?

Or maybe we should focus on pursuing our own journey. We should be humble and openminded to celebrate the diversity of life stages at different ages. "Too early" or "too late" indicates judging, and this is no one's call but your own. If you follow your heart, there could never be one step too early nor one step too late. It's just about right.

Sometimes it takes a lot of courage to live our lives on our own terms. Therefore, not only is it important to do so with courage, it's also important to support others doing so as well. Everyone has their own pace and journey, and we want to support our loved ones to live their life at their own rhythm.

CHAPTER 9

WE CAN'T WRITE OTHERS' EXAMS

———

I am on a flight to Montréal.

I am going to meet Dimi, my nephew, for freshman registration at McGill University and to help him prepare for school. He took an earlier flight, so we will meet up at the airport. His eighteenth birthday is just a few days away.

I can't help but remembering the year when I was eighteen.

He was a strong and adorable baby then, staying with my mom in Kunming, our hometown. It might be hard to imagine a newborn baby staying away from the parents, but my brother and sister-in-law were in the process of moving from Québec to British Columbia and juggling school, jobs, and life as new immigrants in Canada. It's also very common in Chinese culture that grandparents help with bringing up the grandchildren to support the parents.

He stayed with my mom for about three years. For most of the time, my mom was taking care of him. I went to help from time to time. I used to help change his diapers back then, something he might not want me to mention nowadays. I didn't see him again until 2012 when I was in Portland for a business trip. He turned into a quiet teenage boy. He didn't seem to be very close to me or remember a lot about when he was younger. We only reunited when I moved to Canada in 2016.

Today, I am sending him off to university. The plan was that my sister-in-law, my niece, and I would all go, but some things came up and I turned out to be the only parent figure for his registration, prep, and orientation. They will catch up later.

It's quite fascinating how we participate in each other's lives in unexpected ways. For years we weren't really involved in each other's lives, but I turned out to be there for some significant moments without any awkwardness. That feels like family bond to me. The river of time flows endlessly, washing away the marks of many things, as if nothing had happened.

Helping Dimi settle into university takes me further down memory lane. At eighteen years old, I went to university as well.

Today, high school students in China have diversified options after graduation. They may go abroad, take exams developed by their target universities, or take the national exam. In the 2000s, it was conventional to take the path of participating in the national exam and then go to Chinese universities. With few exceptions, the grade one got on the entrance examination for university (*Gao Kao*) would determine which university one could attend. Therefore, it was an intense preparation process, overshadowing almost all three years of the high school life as we only had one shot. Of course, if people are not satisfied with their result, they can retake the exam but in the following year. Trust me, you don't want to relive the last year of high school.

There were four tiers of university, including special schools (art, military, etc.), top-tier schools, first-tier, and second-tier. Other than that, there were many other choices of colleges and institutes but not in the category as university. In terms of the qualifying grade, top-tier schools require the highest among all, while special schools require "special talent" on top of the exam grade. That was the exception: people with higher special talent scores but lower exam scores could still be considered for the special schools. In terms of the final selecting process, special schools select from their applicants first, who presumably had passed the special talent tests beforehand, then the top schools start the selecting process, then the rest follow in respective order. For an individual student, one can apply to 3–5 schools from every tier across China.

It was the first and only time Beijing Broadcasting Institute (BBI, now known as the Communication University of China) set up the test in Kunming, the capital city of Yunnan. Usually, test sites of all kinds of special schools would be set in Chengdu, the capital city of Sichuan Province. It is considered to be the center of Southwest China extensively including Tibet and Qinghai, as well as the Yunnan and Guizhou Plateau.

BBI was known for creating TV, radio, and other media professionals in China, so it's a very niche school with a famous reputation. The alumni are active faces and voices and, more importantly, the hands and brains of all kinds of media across China. In the era of traditional media, TV was the dominant media, so it was easy for young people to dream of being part of it. They could see the alumni and easily visualize their careers, which was very attractive and had a direction. Besides, all the national, provincial, and municipal media were led or managed by the alumni, so it's almost guaranteed that after graduation, one could have a relatively prestigious job under their belt. To put it this way, if you want to be a (famous) TV host, journalist, or producer, you go to BBI. Due to its unique focus, BBI required an additional talent test or interview like other art schools to screen applicants. The test content depended on different majors.

It was criticized that broadcasting was not really a major even by our own professor, but young kids were dreaming of becoming famous broadcasters. Therefore, it was very competitive to get into BBI. It was very common for students to stay updated and prepare for the talent tests months prior, if not a year.

I didn't know that BBI had a test site locally until a week before the application deadline. My dad took me to a friend's, and their daughter was preparing for the most competitive major, Chinese Broadcasting. They suggested that since I've been hosting and giving speeches, maybe I should give it a try for a new major that year, English broadcasting.

Honestly, like many other eighteen-year-olds, I didn't know what I was interested in or passionate about. I knew that I wanted to go to Beijing to study. I knew I wanted to study English. I knew I liked to talk to people. But these were all vague aspirations. So, when I learned about this major, the idea of being an English broadcaster sounded fancy and made my "interest" more tangible.

I consulted my dad about it, as I deem him really smart and someone who always had an answer. He didn't say what I should do or make my choice for me. Instead, he laid out his thoughts and analysis as usual.

"You like giving speeches and even won some awards. So you seem to be good at doing similar things and it seems to satisfy you. When you are not certain about any more things, you can focus on what you are certain about."

He also provided his strategy. Since applying for it wouldn't impact applying to any other tier of schools, I had nothing to lose. So I decided to apply.

My dad was more excited than I was I think. We went to the test site and applied for the major of English broadcasting. Applicants may apply for two majors, so many people did so as one of them can be a backup. After discussing with my dad, I decided if I couldn't make the one I wanted, then I wouldn't settle for anything else. If I couldn't get into English broadcasting, I would not apply for other majors. We met with a lecturer whom I knew about later; the love of her life was from Yunnan, and she fought for the opportunity of recruiting. I completed the first test and was waiting for the next step.

Then I received the notification to go to Beijing for an interview, including a self-introduction, reciting a story, and a Q&A. I asked my friend and mentor Hilary to help me prepare. She was a consultant at Yunnan TV Station then and was teaching English as well. She helped me revise my self-introduction and picked up a story that I could memorize. I thought the Q&A part would be the most difficult as it requires improvising, so we prepared a wide range of questions with answers from a bunch of hot topics on the news to more personal ones. I memorized a lot of different talking points, as big as what my opinion was regarding the political reformation and as small as my favorite food.

I went to her apartment once every week after school for a couple of months to prepare for the test, and my dad always came to pick me up when we were done. All those winter nights I didn't notice much but focused on my preparation. However, I could still clearly visualize the BBQ stand at the entrance of her neighborhood. Every time I finished the class, I could expect that my dad would have ordered a skewer of BBQ tofu for me—warm, puffy, slightly charcoaled, well-seasoned—the best reward after studying during a cold night. Though Kunming was known for its year-round spring weather, it still could be quite chilly on winter evenings. Then we would cycle back home together and chat about the session.

The interview would be videotaped, as marked on the notification, suggesting proper makeup. It was very common that schools prohibited students to wear makeup in China, not mentioning how busy studying could be and that everyone just wanted more sleep if possible, so I had zero experience in putting on makeup. I only had a few days left before leaving for Beijing to do something about it. I had bought a bottle of perfume from the cosmetic store in my neighborhood a while back, so I went to ask the owner to teach me how to put on makeup. He was quite thrilled that I was applying for TV broadcasting as well, saying he would love to see me on TV one day. He taught me the basic knowledge and technique so I could handle myself before the interview. That was when I bought my first foundation, blush, and lipstick ever in my life.

I thought I was ready.

I skipped a mock-up exam for *Gao Kao*, instead taking the train with my dad which was a three-day trip. He didn't preach to me but supported my decision. The last time I had gone to Beijing was the summer of 1988, when my whole family was taking my brother to university. I only could remember the uproarious chirping of cicadas under the washed-blue sky without a thread of clouds.

When we arrived and got out to Beijing Railway Station, I had, for the first time, a visual of what Buddhism referred as *mortal beings*. There were so many people, but their faces were blurry. The city was gray and ready to dilute anyone fresh to blurry face. I didn't remember much about Beijing on that trip but the wind cutting my cheek.

We went to draw for my position in the test right after we checked in the hotel, and I got the second time slot on the first day. I thought I was ready.

When I entered the waiting area, I was shocked by how underdressed I was. Everyone around me was fully dressed up like a real TV broadcaster with professional makeup and hair, just like the *real* deal. They were exchanging the rates of makeup artists they hired and what training program (like it was a thing!) they took. I didn't have much to say. I was wearing a black turtleneck, picked out by myself, and had my hair braided in two braids, by myself.

I couldn't do much, so I tried to concentrate on my prepared content. Without leaving me much time to adjust, my name was called. I stood up and paced to the classroom feeling extraordinarily calm. Maybe I reached my panic quota when I realized how unprepared my appearance was.

I followed the procedure: first I did a self-introduction, then recited a story. The last part was Q&A. I remembered everything Hilary had helped me to prepare. I thought I was ready.

One of the examiners was the lecturer I met back in Kunming, and she asked me an unexpected question.

"Can you sing a song?"

I was startled. It wasn't on the brief of the exam, meaning I didn't prepare for it.

Don't get me wrong, I like singing. I feel like singing when I have my moment. But back then I was focusing on prepared content for a guided exam.

With absolutely no reason, I picked a folk song from my own ethnic minority group. It's about how the world would be without women. The sun could rest, the moon could rest, but the women couldn't, as the fire of the house would go out. There would be no people on the mountain if there were no women. The tone was beautiful, and it was sung in my local dialect that they didn't understand. I only found out after I started that their faces were getting more and more confused. That was it. That should be the end of my journey, my goal, my sort-of-finally-know-what-I-wanted.

No more questions. I was dismissed. None of the content prepared was used. My heart was empty, not feeling much of anything—no regret, no perturbation, no excitement. I prepared as much as I could and did my best. For the unexpected part, I did what I could. No matter what the result would be, I had no regret. In retrospect, when we are put at the crossroads of life, this is probably what we feel the most. The future is far from being seen; the past is as is. The present turns into a Zen meditation-like situation so it feels like deep nothing.

I stepped out into the waiting hall and saw my dad. Because I was the second group, there were still many peers waiting. My dad came up and asked me how it was, especially with the Q&A as it is the biggest variable.

"They asked me to sing a song," I answered stone-faced.

The crowd immediately exploded with surprise all grumbling that it wasn't on the brief. I couldn't stay one second longer, so I just left with my dad.

We spent a few more days in Beijing to relax then went back home. Then everything was just routine: preparing for the *Gao Kao,* applying for schools in the rest of the tiers, then writing the exam. After the final admissions were released on TV, I still couldn't find my name anywhere. I waited and waited, wondering if I had been accepted. That night I had broken dreams of walking on the BBI campus.

It finally dawned on my dad that maybe I should go check the mail at my high school. I cycled across the city to the campus. It was empty and quiet. The security guard didn't even wait for me to get off the bike to tell me that I had a letter from Beijing delivered days ago.

It was the offer letter.

I was going to BBI. After summer vacation, I left home for Beijing. I moved to a new city, opened a new chapter, encountered new people, and stepped into new stories.

That trip was special in so many ways. It decided a major stage of my life. It started all the unanswered questions leading to my self-discovery. It led to many unrelated dots that I waited years to connect. But while living through it, it was just another day.

The flight started to descend. I collected my thoughts and was ready to go.

Today is my turn to support Dimi. He is leaving home to go across North America, open his new chapter, and start his new life. I can only have his back, not hold his hand. I can only until now understand my dad's feeling. Just like how my dad supported me throughout and stepped back—how he gave me the freedom to be myself, trusting me to be able to navigate, yet always being there for me—this is what I could do for Dimi. He may be so excited about it like I used to be, not really noticing how his parents and auntie feel. But I am blessed to be able to experience the bittersweet reality of growing up.

CHAPTER 10

WE GET WHAT WE HAVE

It was a warm Friday afternoon in May, five months after I moved to Canada. Spring was recognized as the best season in Vancouver if you were to ask around. The reputable cherry blossom just had its glory and was about to fade with its unbearable beauty. The seemingly continuous, annoying rain suddenly disappeared. The sun was out, and the sky was constantly washed blue and crystal clear. The temperature raised to a point where you could actually enjoy an afternoon at the Second Beach without sweating. It was also the day I got the job offer I was hoping for among the opportunities I was waiting to hear back from.

I was thrilled.

When the CEO called me asking me to go to the office to sign the contract in about two hours, I was still working on a bouquet at my brother's flower shop. The office was in downtown Vancouver—Gastown, where the famous Steam Clock was located, a must-see for tourists. The flower shop was in Port Moody, which was another city in Metro Vancouver. It usually took forty-five minutes to drive from one to the other. However, I didn't have my driver's license yet, so I had to take the bus. I had dressed very casually as I was working with flowers and moving water around at the shop, so I had to first go back to my brother's house to change, which was in another city, about thirty minutes away from the shop.

I told my brother about the call, and he said, "You should go as soon as possible. I will take care of the shop." So I caught the next bus home. As I walked uphill toward my home, I was in a full-blown hurry and became short of breath. I quickly changed into an above-the-knee dress with French stripes, then picked up my white open-toe high heels, throwing them into my tote, and rushed out for the SkyTrain to Gastown.

The SkyTrain was another special aspect of Vancouver. It connected Metro Vancouver above ground so that you could see the towns outside of the window. I was sitting in the front row during the hour, so I could see new scenes coming toward me. It was like I was heading into my future.

My thoughts were jumping around finding a job during the ride on the SkyTrain. Prior to moving to Canada, I gave myself six months to settle in and kick off building a new life in terms of my career. It was not an easy decision to leave Shanghai; I had friends, a network, and opportunities there. I had worked in public relations, marketing, and business development for about ten years, so I had been approached by all kinds of headhunters all the time with better packages. My career was on the right track, I would say. It didn't seem wise to leave them all behind, and honestly, I wasn't sure at the time if it was a good decision to leave. I wasn't sure what I was going to face. I wasn't sure where I wanted to take my career. What I was sure about was that I had the feeling of being stuck in Shanghai after ten years. I had to shake things up. I had to restart. I needed to get distracted from my depression.

I told myself if I couldn't find a job I liked in six months, I would move back. Although I obtained permanent residency even before I moved, I didn't want to be trapped by it. If things didn't work out, it was just a sunk cost. I would (hopefully) always have the courage to start over. Wise people would say it was lack of planning, and at the time I would have agreed. However, I realized much later that I was a person without a plan, without a road map, who strongly believed that we would get all and only what we should have…and I had to live with it or, more importantly, be grateful and happy about it.

I didn't arrive expecting much. Everyone told me that it was extremely difficult for new immigrants to find jobs here in Vancouver as they "don't have Canadian experience," and it's a relatively small market. A lot of people start with hourly jobs or labor work, which, without local certificates, can be very general experiences that one can't transfer to the next job. According to Immigrant Demographic, Vancouver B.C. by NewtoBC, "6.5 percent of Vancouver's recent immigrants were unemployed in 2015, slightly higher than its total immigrant labor force (5.4 percent) and their Canadian-born counterparts (5.8 percent)." Additionally, "immigrants and recent immigrants represented 41.8 percent and 6.5 percent of the city's labor force respectively, a decline from the corresponding figures of 43.5 percent for total immigrants and 6.9 percent for recent immigrants reported in the NHS 2011."

I didn't do the quantitative research before I came, as I believed that data was just data. Data wouldn't tell me if I belonged to the group of getting a job or not. Either way, it's 100 percent up to me personally. I always had hope. I was okay with potentially getting a more junior job with lower pay as long as it was a job in a bigger business sector that had a scope of work that could be transferred in case I wanted to go back to Shanghai. Frankly speaking, I didn't think I was unrealistic. I set a bottom line for what I was willing to accept from a job, one that I would not change, and this made the decision making much easier.

I first applied for a Chinese media company for the position of marketing manager. My dad was following them on social media and thought they had rich content and could match my experience, so he suggested that I give it a try.

It was mid-February. I applied with my old resume from Shanghai before I participated in the job search training for new immigrants. I received the interview notice the next day, and this to me meant that they were very efficient. The line manager, as well as the founder of the website, interviewed me for about an hour and a half in Chinese. He told me that he would let me know if I qualified for a second interview with other senior managers in a week. When I didn't get the call after a week, I followed up. He told me that they postponed recruitment till the end of February, so they wouldn't have the short list until then. Understandable. When I didn't hear back by the end of February, I followed up again, and he told me to come in for the second interview mid-March.

When I arrived for my second interview, it was with the same person. I was a bit surprised as I thought I was going to meet other senior managers, so I asked about the others. He didn't explain but told me it would be fine just talking to him again. We chatted for another hour and a half. By then, I had a not-so-positive gut feeling about the whole situation. He asked a question about how to promote one of the columns. I thought it was legit as it was in my realm, so I answered with my expertise and experience. He seemed to be satisfied with the answer. And then he pulled out a legal letter.

"Read this," he said.

It was a letter from a person who was featured in their story requesting them to withdraw the report, or else they would sue them for infringement in the United States.

"How would you reply?" he asked. "Would you call them or write a letter?"

"I don't think I am in the position to reply." I found it very unreasonable. "Legal letters should not be dealt with by people other than counselors. I don't think I have the relevant qualifications or the knowledge."

"Just say whatever you feel—your thoughts, your thinking process," he insisted.

I was quite uncomfortable but briefly told him, "Maybe the company should first investigate what happened internally, and then make a plan from then on."

He asked me to draft a reply, and I politely rejected by saying multiple times that legal letters shouldn't be handled by people other than lawyers. He insisted so I said what I could do was just to draft from the perspective of public relations, to manage the impact. I was not let go until I finished writing. It was extremely uncomfortable.

After another week, I received the notice to send them two letters of recommendation. My ex-bosses were very supportive and sent them to me immediately. The founder received the letter and told me he was going back to China and would not be back until the end of March. I got the feeling that this position wasn't important to them, and I had doubts already about working with him as he didn't seem very professional to me.

Then he called me early April to offer me the job.

"However," he continued, "because you don't have any Canadian experience, we will offer you the title of assistant marketing manager. The pay will be cut to 80 percent. But don't worry, you will do the exact same job."

Don't worry? I would do the exact same job with a lower title and pay? Was I hearing this right?

"After a year of probation, if your performance is good, we will promote you and increase your salary," he said confidently.

Although I didn't get the "don't worry" part, the one year of probation period sounded too long and illegal. Even just from a very practical perspective, the pay was not enough to cover a basic life.

"You are new to Canada. You shouldn't expect more than that. Everyone starts like this. This is probably the best you can get. You shouldn't be so picky," he told me.

I didn't have any other opportunities in hand then and was also told "it's good enough to have a job, just settle for now." But after consideration, I turned down the offer. I couldn't bring myself to settle for that. It's not just the pay or title. It was below my bottom line. I wanted a job where I could grow and learn, as well as with potential to transfer if I wanted to go back. I didn't see it in this job. Plus, it didn't feel right to work with this person. I had to have faith in myself.

I then participated in the job search training program for new immigrants run by the government. The best value I found was that I updated my resume to a style that was acceptable in Canada and then uploaded it to Indeed.

In middle April, I received a phone call from my current job to arrange the first interview. It didn't go very well. One of the two founders was late from a previous meeting, and the other one seemed to have about two hundred conference calls going on the same time. I didn't get to spend much time with either of them.

The position was a midlevel executive assistant for a venture capital firm. I found it very attractive as it was a great way to broaden my skill set in a rising industry. The firm funded mostly high tech, financial tech, and clean energy start-ups with about twenty in the portfolio. The super busy founder was challenging me on my background as there would be a lot of technical and analytical information to process.

"I don't have Canadian experience," I said at the end of my self-introduction.

"It doesn't matter." I was slightly surprised hearing that. "Experience can be gained but not the mindset. I need to find the right person with the right mindset."

I suggested that maybe I could be given a test project, as long as it was related directly to the position. He seemed to be dubious. I followed up the next week. His reply was succinct: "Give me some time." I later realized that he was just super busy.

In the meantime, a headhunter called me for a position for one of the biggest companies in Canada. The position was talent attraction specialist, focusing on social media and digital marketing with the capability of working in both English and French. I was quite interested because it was close to my previous experience, and I could sharpen my French. Plus, as a first job, a big corporation could be very convincing. We chatted for about two hours, then he recommended me to his client. He followed up immediately on the first-round interview much faster than I thought. I also openly introduced that I didn't have any Canadian experience again. To my surprise, the marketing director said it was not a problem. I was feeling great.

By the first week of May, both companies invited me for second interviews. The big corporation was arranging my French test, and the venture capital firm invited me for a lunch with the super busy founder and CFO on a Tuesday. The founder was still not convinced and challenged me as to how my new employer could believe in me when every time I switched jobs, I moved to seemingly very different roles. I tried my best to explain my rationale behind every job switch.

By the end of the lunch, we still didn't come up with any way to test my ability to process technology information. I mentioned that I always needed to prepare presentations for different projects that I wasn't entirely familiar with. He finally got inspiration and gave me an assignment to make a company profile of 10–15 PowerPoint slides for a tech start-up they invested in, an EV wireless charging company. I studied the technology and found it very interesting. I made the presentation and sent to him the next day. He confirmed he received it and would talk to his partner on Thursday. Then he called me earlier on the Friday to come in and sign the contract.

* * *

As the SkyTrain approached the Waterfront station, it would go underground like the rest of the subways in the world. Waterfront station is a main transportation hub for Vancouver. Here all the trains, SkyTrains, ferries, and bus stops intertwine. It was about a ten-minute walk from the station to the office, and I was almost late. There were so many tourists on the street that I had to nudge my way through the crowd. A heritage building stands next to the Steam Clock at the end of Cambie Street. Next to it, there were a handful of crisscrossing train tracks. On the elevator, I put on my open-toe high heels, hoping that I wasn't too sweaty or short of breath. The elevator ascended slowly so I was able to smooth my breath. It finally stopped at the top floor, and I was greeted by a colleague. My boss and the CFO came over, and we signed the employment agreement.

I worked there for four years on multiple investments, among which we spent a major chunk of time working on one company until it was sold. During this time, the company funded my master's degree in Business Administration at the Sauder School of Business at the University of British Columbia based on my performance. I was lucky to have had the opportunities, but more importantly, I was so grateful to my boss for believing in and supporting me.

It was not an easy job, but I always felt grateful as there were many harder jobs in the world and many hardworking people. I was a professional woman in Shanghai, and I wanted to work hard to contribute and gain respect, a good reputation, and trust in my new job. In this job, I once stayed on the line with airlines for over ten hours continuously to track a luggage and was able to make it arrive to my boss's last stop of that trip within twenty-four hours. The airline staff told me they've never heard of such a quick fix. I've worked long hours on pitch decks, printing them and making the binder till midnight. I also had to deal with sexual harassment from an investor. I wasn't a stranger to any of these sorts of struggles, and I handled them like a professional.

In retrospect, I was leaning toward the venture capital firm early on in the process of recruitment. I used to work in both big corporations and start-ups because I liked the vibe and autonomy of start-ups. Although the big company seemed great and very promising, although I had been challenged many times even before I started in the venture capital firm, although there was such a steep learning curve, my heart wanted to go to the venture capital firm. I was blessed to have the chance to follow my heart. I was so grateful to have gotten what I wanted. This job meant so much to me. It was my first job after arriving in a new country. It fulfilled my willingness to achieve a master's degree. It opened more doors for me. It was also where I met the love of my life. I couldn't thank my boss enough.

My friend used to say that he thought I would have a happy life because I always took the harder path. I wasn't sure. How could one gain happiness by taking a harder path? If it's so difficult every day, where would happiness lay out? I asked him the question after I signed the offer.

"Maybe the feeling of happiness will be more intense due to having put more into the harder path," he thought and replied.

Maybe yes, maybe no.

Or maybe, the path we take is what we are supposed to take. It leads to where you are supposed to be.

CHAPTER 11

MIGHT AS WELL JUST DANCE

Joy, my niece, had a dance performance last Sunday. It was the year-end showcase for the dance school she had been going to. I went to help to do her makeup and watched the whole show. From a chain of toddlers led by the teacher and not doing much other than just coming and going up and down the stage to high school dancers showing quite a professional performance; from street dance to jazz; from modern ballet and to musical, I found it truly enjoyable. There were more girls than boys, and most boys were doing street dance. As it's a showcase, all the performances were grouped by different classes, the size of which varied from a handful to a dozen of dancers.

To my surprise, they were not all very uniform or coherent, and a lot of the dancers did not have the "conventional" dancer body—thin and well proportioned. Many of them were plump and didn't necessarily have long limbs, small heads, or the ideal body measurements, which I'd heard about so much when I was studying dance. However, they were all enjoying themselves. I was quite touched watching how they all indulged in dancing.

Joy has been dancing with this school for over five years. She once switched to a more "traditional" school with a similar style to China. My sister-in-law told me that the training was very rigorous and she was heavily stressed. Even the makeup had to be done by one single teacher before any performance. Joy got really nervous and even more so as she didn't enjoy the classical dance. So she asked to switch back to the current school and continued jazz.

When listening to my sister-in-law talk about Joy's dance journey, I remembered my own.

My mom sent me to a very famous local dance club called Little Peacock when I was about four or five years old. The instructor was Mr. Zhang Laishan, who was a professional dancer and an excellent teacher. The dance studio was in the exhibition center. The wall was off-white and painted mint green to about one meter above the floor. The double doors were painted in light yellow with glasses inlaid as the parents were tall enough to look from the outside, but the kids were too short to look out from the inside so we couldn't get distracted.

Once toward the end of the class, we were stretching facing down on the floor, rolling the legs while using our head to reach our feet. I always suffered from cambré (body arch) as my flexibility was quite bad, so I started to drift. I got distracted by the kid behind me as I lifted my head to reach my feet, and I could see her. Then I started to distract her by chatting with her. Not only did I not focus on my own training, but I also interrupted other kids. Everything was seen by my mom standing outside, waiting to pick me up after class. I was punished when we got home.

With the limit of my own body, my dance hobby didn't go much further. It wasn't even a hobby; I didn't really enjoy it. I danced on and off through my childhood until I was ten, then I started to play piano. After entering high school, all hobbies were abandoned to make room for the entrance examination for university. However, I needed an outlet from the intense studying. One day, my dad came home telling me one of his colleagues was learning ballet from an instructor who looked only forty-years-old but was actually over sixty. My dad suggested if I still wanted to dance, this could be a great opportunity. It was very rare in 1999 for adults to practice ballet as a hobby. No belly dance either. This was even before the yoga fever. Latin dance, however, was very popular then.

I was curious and told my bestie in high school, Yolanda. We both liked classical music as well as dancing. We decided to sign up together. We went twice a week in the evening after school, and the classes were even more fun because we did them together. We then performed modern ballet at the annual school party to the music of *Chariots of Fire.* Being total amateurs and still not being very flexible, we both put on toe shoes and completed the performance.

Ballet became an escape from my routine high school life. I was less concerned about my body proportion, my flexibility, and technique than when I was younger. It was like chasing the stars: though I would never be able to touch it, I was covered with the gentle star lights.

After entering university, we had a mandatory course on body shaping as part of our training to be TV presenters after graduation. It wasn't dancing, but at least I got to keep some basic practice to keep my body active. Then I moved to Shanghai after graduation, starting a new job and a new life there. For about three or four years, I didn't dance much except while clubbing with friends. I could still feel myself yearning for dance. Maybe it was in my blood. Whenever I felt I needed to express myself, I would always sing and dance.

Belly dance showed up as a coincidence in 2009. I went back to my hometown, Kunming, after breaking up with the ex who threatened to burn my apartment down. I had much more time on my hands and was looking for some activities. My cousin was learning belly dance from a very young instructor who later became our friend. I've been belly dancing since then.

Ironically, I picked up belly dance completely based on the stereotype: I thought it was a feminine dance, which I hoped to learn to make myself look more attractive. When you think of belly dancing, what image comes to mind? Maybe a sexy woman wearing classical two-pieces covering almost nothing of her body, stretching and posing with strong female distinct and more importantly, eroticism...such a cliché.

Luckily, after years of practicing and with the help of my mentor Estella, a great dancer and teacher whom I met after I moved back to Shanghai, I realized there was so much more than the female symbolism in this dance, which she redefined as oriental dance. My native English-speaking friend told me that *oriental* is a term also deemed as biased or even racist. But in the Chinese language, belly dance stresses the body and physical expression while oriental dance carries a meaning of the origin of the dance. That's why my mentor used it and promoted the concept.

In its long history of developing, oriental dance has been through a lot of pride and prejudice. The advent of dance has strong spiritual aspects, and dance is so much more than just body movement. It's the same situation with oriental dance, a.k.a. belly dance. It is considered one of the oldest dance forms on earth, but no one knows for sure where it came from.

Unlike many Western dance forms, the focus of the dance was isolated to the torso muscles, rather than movements of the limbs. Although some of these isolations appeared similar to the isolations used in jazz or ballet, they are sometimes driven differently and have a different feeling or emphasis. Similar to most folk dances, there is no universal naming scheme for belly dance movements.

We can definitely see the link among all the dance forms along the Silk Road. It is amazing how human beings explored the possibility to change their lives along the Silk Road, and along the way they shared their dance traditions.

According to the Encyclopedia Britannica, in Dunhuang Frescoes in China, the signature image, Fei Tian (meaning flying in the sky), was very similar to the Green Tara of Hinduism, a goddess who helped people get out of sorrow. Going back to the Chinese character of dance, it could be legitimate; after all, dance was originally a ceremonial component as a spiritual expression of our ancestors' lives.

A well-known myth which used to be my misunderstanding of this dance was gender. This myth claimed that oriental dance was for women only and that men should not do it. But in the Middle East, it is a basic part of their dance movement vocabulary and is a part of everyday life for everyone—women, men, and children. It is the Egyptian equivalent to how the typical Americans may dance in a club or at a party; it is just the way they dance. It is a natural expression of the body reacting to a certain type of music and rhythm. The same as some other everlasting beauty profoundly connected with the universe, spirit, and human beings, oriental dance is an art deeply mistaken and misunderstood.

Since the first class I walked into, belly dancing brought me what I was looking for. I was able to dance with feminine expression and my shape was getting better. But most of all, it enabled me to truly dance for myself. It enabled me to focus on the connection between myself and the music, between my body and my mind, rather than focus on techniques and performance.

In the beginning of my dancing journey when I was younger, I was too nervous and self-conscious to enjoy the dance. But belly dancing taught me how to feel satisfied with myself no matter what and to just enjoy dancing. I have never really liked meditation in the sense of sitting still for hours, and instead I use dancing as a sort of meditation. Along the journey I learned more about what my body wants, what my heart wants. Lucky ones may have this figured out at the very beginning, but this was my journey, where I cherish it so, so much.

One thing I remember very vividly was when I was watching the mentor of my mentor, in her late sixties, dance so comfortably and beautifully when she was visiting our class. It made me believe that no matter how old I was, no matter if I had a dance partner, no matter how my flexibility was, I could keep dancing. We might as well just dance from dawn to dusk.

CHAPTER 12

BLUE

It was just another day in the English class for new immigrants.

I like going to classes. I like the atmosphere of a classroom and the feeling of being a student. When I first arrived in Vancouver, I was helping my brother with his flower shop but didn't go there every day. I found out that there were several free programs for new immigrants such as job search training and English language education to help people settling in. I also thought of it as a good way to start building a social network as well, so I registered for the English class.

The instructor organized her course by different topics each month, and this month the topic was careers. The breakout task that day was to pick five occupations among the list provided by the instructor and have one-on-one dialogue about the pros and cons of each one. I was paired with Hose.

I had actually noticed her at the beginning of our class. Her eyes were the first thing that caught my attention. They were warm gray and in perfect size proportional to her face. She was wearing a hijab which made her eyes even more outstanding and her face even smaller. Her slightly pale face showed a delicate beauty that was almost fragile.

I learned from the self-introduction in the first class that she was from Afghanistan and had moved here about a year ago for marriage. Her English was quite good, and she was always quick to volunteer answers during class. When we were giving presentations on the impact of globalization, she provided very good points of view on the impact of media. I was quite impressed not only by her language ability but also her thoughtfulness.

We said hello and moved to a corner of the classroom and started to scan through a few occupations, landing on construction workers.

"The cons of this occupation could be that the working environment is dangerous and chaotic," I said.

She replied, "Oh, yes, my husband used to be a construction worker. The pay was good, but he took showers twice a day. He was so dirty when he came home. Thank God he quit two months ago. Now he is a salesman."

"Not bad, it's a big transition though."

"Yes, he is very good at sales! Actually, he doesn't look like a construction man. He is not very rough. Let me show you his picture!" She pulled out her smart phone, and I took a look. He looked quite decent. Then I found her smiling at the picture. *Ah, she must like him a lot*, I thought.

"You two seem so in love. How long have you been married?"

"My story is very unique. The real marriage has been for about a year. I've been waiting for four years to come here." She was a little timid.

"Oh, really? Tell me!" I was immediately curious.

"We had never met each other when we were engaged. It was when his sister got married to my cousin, my now parents-in-law and my sister-in-law came to Afghanistan from Canada to participate in the wedding ceremony. They thought I was beautiful at first sight, so they put pictures of their three sons on the computer screen for me to choose."

She continued on with her story. "I was quite reluctant, but my parents accepted it. His sister said, 'Choose my youngest brother. He is a nice man.' He is also very good looking, so I accepted it and got engaged. Although it was an arrangement by my parents, I was very happy after getting married. Of course, there are problems in our marriage. However, compared with the marriage of free love, we can blame our parents and turn to our mothers to solve the problems." She giggled.

"And when was this?" I was already a bit startled.

"When I was eighteen. I am twenty-five now. We've been contacting each other over the phone since. We kept talking and talking for about a year, then he came to Afghanistan and we had the ceremony…"

"And that was the first time you met each other in person?"

"Yes, but we'd been talking and FaceTiming, so it was like a long-distance relationship."

"…Umm, have you ever had a boyfriend before?"

"No, he never had girlfriend either. Let me show you the engagement party and wedding photos."

I was surprised to find that she wasn't wearing a hijab in any of the photos. Her hair was brown and silky, all exposed. Her dresses were all western style, showing her round shoulders and arms and her beautiful skin color as well.

"You were not wearing a hijab?" The question burst from me suddenly.

"No. My husband is a very devout Muslim, prays five times a day. He fasts strictly during Ramadan. So he hopes that I wear a hijab and long-sleeved shirts and trousers. He hopes that his wife is devout too. In fact, after I came to Canada, I paid closer attention to my faith. I didn't do this to prove anything to anyone else, and I don't care what others think. I did it for my own Allah. I wanted to please him."

"Did your husband grow up in Afghanistan?"

"No, he came to Canada when he was nine with his family. He grew up here, but he is the most devout person I've ever seen!"

"So, when you were waiting to move to Canada, were you a student then?"

"No, actually, I had passed the economics entrance examination of college, but my husband told me to focus on learning English. He said, 'Don't go to college.' I really wanted to work, but my family didn't let me. My parents said, 'We can support you.' After the engagement, my husband said he can support me. No one let me work." Her eyes were not twinkling as much as when she was talking about her marriage. Her face dimmed down a bit.

I didn't know what to say, so I asked perfunctorily, "Do you live far from here?"

"Quite far, so I need to be picked up. Usually I will walk to the bus stop and meet up with my father-in-law, and he will drive me home."

"Oh, you live together!"

"Yes, we are a big family." She was smiling, "You can't even imagine. My in-laws, my mother-in-law's mom, my husband's sister, and her husband and kid, my husband's two brothers…nine of us."

"That is a big family. It must be a big house."

"Yes, nine bedrooms! We just moved into this big house."

"Does your husband enjoy living with the big family?"

"He thinks family is very important, so he never thought about moving out…I don't like it. It's not very convenient. His sister and mom always intrude on our life, you know?" Her smile finally faded away.

"So…moving out could solve the problem." I started to feel agitated.

"His parents are so stupid! They think I stole their son, so they want to punish me." She suddenly got heated.

"What? Punish?"

"They sometimes take away my cell phone and won't let me talk to my parents or tell them about my life here. Sometimes when my husband and I go out for dinner, my mother-in-law will get really upset. She will lose her temper and ask why he didn't take her. They think he is their son first, then my husband. Everything related to me should be put second. His sister is always jealous and pointing fingers at me. They used to be close, so she blames me for stealing her younger brother."

"I'm sorry, but didn't you tell me earlier that they chose you?" I got more agitated and started to feel powerless.

"Yes! So I'm just not happy. Why do they do this? They think I'm disobedient and will talk behind their back. They think I am no longer the little girl they picked, always listening to them. They won't let me work either. They think that once I have income, my husband will obey me more. But I was only eighteen years old. Of course, I didn't know anything. Now that I'm grown up, I have my own ideas. No one can force me to do what I don't want to do."

"Have you talked to your husband?"

"Yes, and he said that family is very important to him. No matter what dispute there is, he will stand by their side. Otherwise, both sides will get hurt. I am very unhappy. There are many problems in our marriage. The biggest problem is his family. There is not a single day that I don't want to leave the house. I have been enduring it, and it's hard to bear it." She was crying and was a different person from when we first started chatting.

"Do you have friends here?" I had problems even concentrating on breathing.

She shook her head, quietly wiping her tears. Nobody noticed that our conversation had been sidetracked for a long time.

"They agreed to let you come to English class...?" I couldn't think of any other questions that would be okay to ask out loud.

"It's a basic survival skill. They always told me not to continue to study. I said that unless I was pregnant and had a baby, I would continue to learn English. I always felt that I didn't go to school enough. I like school."

"Pregnancy and having a baby can be more stressful though..."

"Yes, I don't know. I don't know when I am going to have kids and take care of kids. Could you imagine my life like this? I usually appear quite happy..."

"Everyone has pain inside."

"You are right. No matter how happy a heart is, there is a sad side. If I write a book about my story, it will be interesting." She forced a smile.

"You want to write a book? Just try, just start writing." Maybe this was a light I could offer her.

"No, I can't. I can't do it anymore..." she mumbled gloomily. "I used to love poems. I always tried to write poems when I was in school...then I stopped going to school, and I didn't have the energy, so I lost my talent. I lost this talent."

"Writing poems is good. You can keep trying." I was drowned in deeper sorrow.

"No, I don't have the talent anymore..."

I hesitated for a long time. "How about you save my number so you can talk to me anytime you want to."

She agreed.

However, she never texted me.

CHAPTER 13

SECRET

It was just past 10 a.m. on a Saturday. John walked into the store as usual buying a bouquet that cost around seven dollars. He was not tall but always well dressed. His hair was gelled up perfectly in place, and he wore the same long black wool coat as always. His black scarf had the end tucked up in the coat and a pair of black trousers with matching brogues. His outfit was not at all like a casual weekend outfit but was rather very old fashioned. He was politely chitchatting with me while I was wrapping his bouquet, then he picked up the bouquet, bowing slightly to say goodbye. Ding dong, he pushed the door and walked out.

Other than that, the business was very unpredictable on Saturdays. My brother's flower shop was located in Port Moody, a very small town in Metro Vancouver on the only shopping street in town for over forty years. My brother bought it about a year before I moved to Canada. We had a lot of old patrons who knew the previous owner and still kept coming to the shop on their regular schedule. John was one of them, and he always showed up on Saturday mornings. Sometimes we got so busy that we couldn't stop wrapping flowers, and sometimes nobody would drop by after John.

My routine on Saturday was just changing the water and trimming the stems of the flowers. I never knew what would come my way on Saturdays at the flower shop, but sometimes it was exactly what I needed.

Around 11 a.m., an old Caucasian gentleman walked in. He was about 6"2', and his hair was all gray but silky and shiny. He was walking with a walking stick and seemed to have mobility issues. He was a little short of breath, and his cheeks were slightly ruby. He was also quite paunchy, so when he was walking, it was like a mountain moving forward. Our store suddenly seemed too crowded.

"Good morning, sir. How can I help you today?" I walked up toward him from the back of the store.

"Hi," he said gasping loudly. "Today is my wife's birthday. I would like to have a small bouquet, you know, that can put on your clothes."

"Oh, you mean you want to pin it on the clothes?"

"Yes, that." With a gasp, "Better with white orchid and red rose."

"Sure, let me double-check if we have the flowers." I quickly checked and brought back a corsage. "You would like to have something like this, right? A corsage."

"Ah, yes. Corsage."

"You want it now or would you prefer to pick it up later?" This type of request was usually made on order.

"I have all the time in the world. I can wait. Perfect, I will need a card as well, so I can write while waiting."

"Sure thing. Let me grab you the card!" I briefed my brother to make the corsage and picked up a card for him. He was happy with it and started writing.

When he had finished with the card, my brother was still working on his corsage, so I began chatting with him to keep him feeling welcomed. Naturally, I asked about his wife and how many years they've been married.

"Forty-four years! You bet. I will come again next month, our wedding anniversary."

"Oh my god! Please tell me your secret." I didn't stop the work in my hands.

"We have an ending line: alright, darling. No matter what we are talking about or disputing about, that is my last line. She is a smart woman. She knows what she is doing. Why should I argue with her? We never bring fights with us to bed. You got to let go at the end of the day." I started to concentrate.

"Can't be that easy, right? Forty-four years. How can you solve the problems with this every time?" I was quite dubious. First, it sounded like a compromise or a patch-up. I thought continually comprising or disregarding the feeling could only lead to feeling somewhat dead inside. Also, forty-four years of marriage…could a relationship last so long with such a simple secret?

"I am a businessman." He seemed to have spotted my doubts. "My company had sixty-five employees. I can tell if I am going to get along with someone by just walking from the door to this table. My wife is a professional woman. She is an accountant. She is sharp—still working now! So I know she has a reason."

He totally cheered up talking about her. "Like once her ex-boss asked her to do something. After she listened to it and didn't even lift her head but said, 'This won't work,' the ex-boss then backed down. It turned out to not work. But her ex-boss has passed away. Now it's his daughter who took over the company, but she is out all the time so my wife is taking care of the company." It was definitely a diamond-cutting-diamond situation.

"Still working? Mind if I ask if you have retired?"

"Oh yes, I am seventy years old. I had four back surgeries. I can't work anymore. We were doing greenhouse equipment. I needed a good body."

"My god, what? Four operations?" I was so impressed with his resilience, not expecting it could be exceeded.

"I am no longer very mobile. But I am not sad! If I complain about having back surgeries in the hospital, the next guy in may be missing an arm or a leg. Then I think about myself: I can still move, so I have nothing to complain about. If I think about how I may die one day, then I even have less to be sad about. My doctor told me if I am upset, just go to the toilet, pull off a piece of paper, write down the date—for example, February 27 is a bad day—then flush it. Trust me you will feel so much better."

"Wow you've seen it through. You have your own business. Your wife is working. Do you have any kids?"

"I have six daughters. They all live in different places and have decent lives. I stopped giving them money from the second semester of the first year of college. They always worked very hard during their breaks. You will only respect the money you make. Now kids are all like, 'I want a BMW because Billy next door has one.' Ugh." He rolled his eyes.

"That is so awesome! Your education seemed very successful."

"I think it's because of their mom. My wife had cancer twice. The first time she was diagnosed, she told me, 'If I can come home from the hospital, I will take the accounting test and become a CPA [Certified Public Accountant].' I couldn't do anything but just comfort her. Then she came home from the hospital, and she immediately registered with two schools and studied full time all day long. Our daughters were doing homework and seeing their mom work side by side with them under the lamp. Of course they were very encouraged too. My wife told them, 'The reason I am working so hard now is that I didn't work hard enough when I should have.' Then she continued to work after her second recovery from cancer."

"Leading by example is the best." I was again amazed.

"I know, she is an amazing woman…" He didn't seem to finish recalling.

My mind was drifting away a bit. I had a few relationships but none of them had so much faith. It was very inspiring to see a lived example of a good relationship like his. I believed in true love, but I wasn't too sure about relationships. I just couldn't picture how two people could live through the mundane day-to-day life. Even during my most profound relationship with XM, I never had the faith that it would work because of the practicality issues. Back then, I always thought I should take care of my problems, or maybe I would never be able to trust anyone enough to share my problems. I felt isolated even in a relationship. I wanted the deep connection but couldn't seem to make it happen. Though I wasn't sure if it was me or if it was just not the right person, I never gave up on finding true love.

I admired how they managed their relationship from what I had heard. Though this gentleman's secret seemed over simplified, it actually contained more aspects. It had a precondition that two people treated each other equally and respectfully. They didn't disregard each other's capability, talents, or opinions. They were at least willing to listen to and understand each other's perspective and had no problem giving up their position but kept their interest. Like the first thing I learned in my negotiation course: never negotiate for position. Negotiate for interest. More importantly, they supported each other. In a safe, respectful, and equal relationship, my problems can be our problems, just as theirs can be because we are in this together.

At that time, my brother completed the corsage. He walked over and handed it to him. He was very happy with the purple orchid and red spray rose. I thanked him and processed the payment.

"Don't forget to order before your anniversary!"

"Absolutely! Our wedding anniversary is March 19. I usually get her two dozen red roses. But I will let you know beforehand. Bye!"

"Have a good dinner!"

CHAPTER 14

THE CAT BO LI

Sometimes, I really hate different time zones.

"Bo Li is gone." I read this message in our group chat in the morning. It was sent by Ben at 2:39 a.m. my time, which was 5:39 p.m. for him. If it weren't for the time difference, we could have at least talked about it sooner.

Bo Li didn't wait for me.

My plan was to go back to China in the summer of 2020, as I hadn't been back for three years. She lived with my friend Ben in Shanghai, so I would definitely be able see her.

She wasn't even my cat.

I lived with her for about a year in 2015. I moved back to Shanghai from New York and was uncertain about my move to Canada. Ben was the friend who was kind enough to let me stay at his place for the time being. That's how I had the chance to stay with her for about a year. It's his cat, and back then, he had a dog as well, Le Le.

At the beginning, I wasn't a big fan of hers, nor of Le Le's.

My cat ran away when I was six, jumping out of the window of our apartment on the sixth floor. I watched her run away lamely after jumping from the window. She disappeared and never returned. Then I lost my dog when I was eight. He was poisoned at my mom's friend's yard where we entrusted him to them while we were out of town for a weekend trip. Since then, I never had any pets. It was too painful to have them just to lose them like that. I would say I had PTSD, the P standing for "Pet."

Then I moved around from Kunming to Beijing, then to Shanghai, then to New York, then to Shanghai, then to Vancouver. I couldn't afford to get attached to another pet, so I kept my distance from Bo Li and Le Le. I did not walk Le Le. I rarely reached out to Bo Li to hug her.

Le Le was always bouncy, clingy, and jolly. He would make silly mistakes and get told off but would still stay bouncy, clingy, and jolly. Different from Le Le, Bo Li was quite nonchalant, just like other cats. She was mature, quiet, and slow. She was either wandering around the apartment slowly, staying put, or looking at Le Le as if he was an idiot. Ben adopted her from someone and moved to Shanghai with both of them. It took a while for Bo Li to really get along with Ben or Le Le. She was traumatized by her previous owner, so she didn't get close to us much. This made her different from other cats. I remember Ben telling me that, different from other cats, she hated getting into bags, boxes, or anything trap like. We thought she had claustrophobia.

"How did she go?" I messaged back 9:37 a.m. my time, hoping Ben didn't go to sleep yet.

"Heart failure. She was already gone by the time she arrived at the hospital."

I had always been concerned about her health. She was quite chubby, so she moved slowly. She was a British Shorthair, so we could tell she was quite fully built but she was very beautiful and very cute.

I used to travel a lot when I was staying with Ben. When I was packing up, she would come in, quickly identify the most expensive item or my favorite outfit then go straight up and lay on it, melting like a lump of cream. Sometimes I found it both funny and annoying as she was too chubby to clean her butt, like cats usually do, and she would leave stains on my expensive clothes. I think on the inside, she was a fashionista.

"I am so sorry you have to go through this. What did the doctor say? I remember she was fourteen?"

"A little over ten. I didn't get the chance to experience her last minute. My boyfriend was home. When I rushed to the hospital, and she was gone. She was all normal one second earlier, then started to vomit, then had incontinence and frothing at the mouth. When he held her getting into the cab, she was already gone."

"What's next? How is Le Le reacting? Does he even realize?" We always thought Le Le was a bit silly.

"She will be cremated. I can keep her paw print and a bit of hair. They can make a charm from her ashes. Le Le was very agitated when she passed out according to my boyfriend."

"How is he now?"

He sent me a picture with Le Le laying listlessly on the coach, looking really sad.

"He will be even more sensitive to the loss as he only had Ben and Bo Li," my other friend in the group, Edward, replied.

Ben replied, "The small cat was sad too, she can't stop crying." The small cat was adopted after I left. "She used to hold Bo Li to sleep, but she was snuggling with us the whole evening."

"I can only imagine if no one was there when it all happened. You would have gone mad if she had been alone. At least someone was on spot to deal with it," I said.

"When I rushed into the hospital, people were pointing to the room down the hall. I was okay when I was there." Ben was a very unruffled guy who didn't show much of his feelings, always grounded and calm. "I just sobbed when I was closing her eyes with my fingers but wailed like hell when I got home though."

I felt for him. Even for me, as a friend who just lived with her for only a year, it was hard enough to swallow. But Bo Li meant so much more than that to me.

During my darkest times—those pitch-black nights when I couldn't fall asleep and I was howling and crying, those times I was home alone and felt completely lost, those moments I wanted to destroy myself to stop the pain—it was Bo Li who was by my side. Her purr was so soothing and reassuring that it actually felt like meditation. She felt like someone who had the biggest heart in the world. She would just crawl up to my lap or my bed and melt next to me, warm and heavy, staying quiet by my side. Without saying anything or doing much, without questioning or judging, without offering futile comfort or dismissing my feelings, she was just being.

Just being…

The idea of just being present rarely occurs to us in situations like these. Most of the time, with our loved ones, feeling such great empathy, we almost can't bear to watch them in be pain or "make mistakes." We can't resist the idea of "I know how I can help," even obsessed with the idea of "we can do something."

Can we?

We usually feel like we need to say something or do something immediately. We feel like asking questions or offering comfort to be empathetic and to problem solve, but we can sometimes end up judging and dismissing their feelings when we get so caught in the urge of helping. What this might end up satisfying instead is our need to be useful rather than focusing on the other person's problem. Being aware of this possibility can prevent us from jumping right into problem-solving mode.

Taking a step back, maybe the best we can do is to let go of the twisted illusion that we always know what to do, and just be there for them.

That is what Bo Li showed me, and I found that I started to be quieter when I listening to my loved ones. I was no longer trying to provide an immediate answer to their questions but was just listening, being. Because in my difficult times, I realized those who cared for me would have my back but not always hold my hand.

I learned that I have my own journey at my own pace, and I was lucky enough that they were there. I understood that we each have a different purpose and path.

Just being is so simple yet so powerful. As this book draws to a close, I hope it will provide some power and support to whoever is reading it.

The journey to our true self is not a one-time thing. It's a lifelong spiral, a journey on an often tortuous path aiming to progress ever upwards.

ACKNOWLEDGMENTS

Writing is a lonely wrestle with oneself.

No matter how large the audience around the ring, it is always a battle that one takes with the heart. And most of the time, there is no one who is even watching.

This sounds like the journey of finding your true self—like life, like those dark nights when we question ourselves.

Therefore, I can't say enough about how much I appreciate each and every one of you who have been on this journey with me, supporting me, talking to me, encouraging me, and inspiring me!

You were there during the events in this book. You were there when I launched this book. For many years to come, you will be there as well. And this book will always be there for you, too.

Thank you for believing in me.

In no particular order, thanks to:

Raymond Smith, Eric Koester, Irene Han, Jaclyn Liu, Rayna Yu, Wenyi Liang, Ann Yuu, Bao Chengjie, Anny Chen, Angel Cheung, Libby Minjun Qian, Gabrielle Xiangyuan Kong, Michelle Sun, Ava Yu Schandorff, Deng Ling, Terri Nakamura, Richard Bos, Maria Kilina, Eva Sun, Yang Jing,

Tao Zi, Meng Shu, Yan Chen, Mark Bayley, Sivan Shen, Emily Fu, Rock Ma, Calvin He, Dong Yaoyue, Julie Wu, Shi Qiu, Kexin Sun, Beibei Bao, Sai Kit Luk, Heather Hay, Andrew Ng, Vivian Zhou, Song Jianqiang, Lei Qing, Susie Ni, Jojo Sun, Lyu Mengyang, Qiao Zhi, Ji Wenlong, Xiling Gu, Rachel Hayek, Tianying Huang, Xiaozhuo Wu, Wendy Mann, Li Yang, Hazel de Burgh, Julian Bigi, Zhang Ying, Yang Shu, Li Binxin, Mengting Gao, Wan Lin, Frank Zhong, Ammann, Hani Lee, Alice Hopkins, Wayne Rawcliffe, Terry Boyle McDougall, Fu Yunchong, Zhao Xiuhong, Lyn Lu, Chen Chengji, Yaxuan Lei

Frans Tjallingii, Tuo Su, Jo Xu, Yuan Gao, Jian Yan Chen, Fenway Fan, Gao Jiayi, Chen Chun, Grace Shao, Song Xiao, Francis Lam, Clare Li, Sophia Ma, More Tong, Tina Dong, Shiyao Li, Yun Zhang, Suzanne Muir, Neila Padagas, Sonia Sehra, Yanan Zhang, Calvin Ma, Dimitri Yang, Tian Ji Wu, Maria Z Qian, Xiao Qunhua, Mingyang Sun, Marc van der Chijs, Haiyi Yin, Zefeng Liu, Jenny Chen, Ash Anwar, John Kim, Yoyo Mai, Wendy Yv, Sophia Luan, Julia Yv, Chen Meng, Zhu Yuan, Gong Ting, Wang Jiayi, Wu Yaoyao, Emin Kasapoglu, Guo Rongjun, Molly Lee, Evan Fu, Wang Zhe, Vivian Chen, Li Jing, Tina Bao, Yang Shuyan, Zhu Qiulin, Sherry Xue, Chen Yifei, Nancy Yang, Wang Mo, Fu Lei, Ben Zheng, Triston Lee, Yang Kegong, Miharu Tian, Fang Jun, Lu Yuan, Tina Zhang, Li Miaosheng, Jeremy Moorhouse, Frank Christiaens

I would also like to extend my gratitude to my editors and the NDP team, without whom this book would never be where it is today.

APPENDIX

CHAPTER 5
World Health Organization. Violence Against Women, Key Facts. Accessed March 9, 2021.
https://www.who.int/news-room/fact-sheets/detail/violence-against-women

UN Women, Facts and Figures: Ending Violence against Women, 2020.
Intensification of Efforts to Eliminate All Forms of Violence against Women: Report of the Secretary-General (2020), pg.4.
https://www.unwomen.org/en/digital-library/publications/2020/07/a-75-274-sg-report-ending-violence-against-women-and-girls

CHAPTER 7
Merriam-Webster. s.v. "Epiphany." Accessed March 9, 2021.
http://merriam-webster.com/dictionary/epiphany.

CHAPTER 10
Immigrant Demographics Vancouver. B.C. 2018.
https://newtobc.ca/wp-content/uploads/2013/07/Vancouver-Immigrant-Demographic-Profile-2018.pdf

CHAPTER 11
Britannica, T. Editors of Encyclopaedia. "Silk Road." Encyclopedia Britannica. Accessed September 29, 2020.
https://www.britannica.com/topic/Silk-Road-trade-route.

www.ingramcontent.com/pod-product-compliance
Lightning Source LLC
LaVergne TN
LVHW011841060526
838200LV00054B/4124